Communicating Across Cultures

The key to

successful

international

business

communication

howto books

Every effort has been made to identify and acknowledge the
sources of the material quoted throughout this book. The author
and publishers apologise for any errors or omissions, and would
be grateful to be notified of any corrections that should appear in
any reprint or new edition.

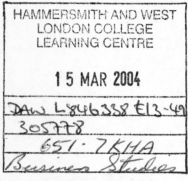
First published in 2003 by
How To Books Ltd, 3 Newtec Place,
Magdalen Road, Oxford OX4 1RE. United Kingdom.
Tel: (01865) 793806. Fax: (01865) 248780.
email: info@howtobooks.co.uk
http://www.howtobooks.co.uk

British Library Cataloguing in Publication Data
A catalogue record for this book is available from the British
Library

Cover design by Baseline Arts Ltd, Oxford
Produced for How To Books by Deer Park Productions
Typeset by PDQ Typesetting, Newcastle-under-Lyme, Staffs.
Printed and bound by Cromwell Press, Trowbridge, Wiltshire.

NOTE: The material contained in this book is set out in good
faith for general guidance and no liability can be accepted
for loss or expense incurred as a result of relying in particular
circumstances on statements made in the book. The laws and
regulations are complex and liable to change, and readers should
check the current position with the relevant authorities before
making personal arrangements.

Communicating Across Cultures

Thank you for buying one of our books. We hope you'll find the book interesting, and that it will help enhance your business relationships when you are travelling abroad or working with other cultures at home.

Please do also give us your feedback so we can go on making books that you want to read. If there's anything you particularly liked about this book – or you have suggestions about how it could be improved in the future – email us on info@howtobooks.co.uk

The Publishers
www.howtobooks.co.uk

howtobooks

Please send for a free copy of the latest catalogue:

How To Books
3 Newtec Place, Magdalen Road,
Oxford OX4 1RE, United Kingdom
email: info@howtobooks.co.uk
http://www.howtobooks.co.uk

Contents

About the Authors   ix
Preface   xiii

PART 1 Bridging the Communication Gap   1

1. **Why this book**   3

These days cross-border travel is commonplace, whether for business or pleasure, and cultural diversity is in our midst. Yet our understanding of other cultures has lagged behind our access to them. The consequences can be serious. This chapter sets the scene for the insights that are to follow, with examples of the miscommunication that commonly occurs between people whose thinking is limited by their own national borders.

2. **Why speaking louder and slower doesn't work**   9

When we cannot make ourselves understood, we speak louder and slower. In English. But there's much more to effective communication than that technique, or even our efforts to fit in with the limited vocabulary of foreigners. This chapter presents the 10 keys to connecting with people whose first language is not English, and recalls the classic business blunders of multinational firms who should have known better.

3. **East is East and West is West**   22

The diversity in attitudes to social behaviour, from nation to nation, can cause great friction. And yet, in matters of face-saving there are similarities the world over. This chapter identifies those similarities as well as defining the differences between East and West, for example in their typical approach to timekeeping.

4. East/West influences on thinking   30

*Extending the theme of the previous chapter, this one
explores how culture determines our personal values and
reasoning styles, and therefore our behaviour. Read
about the surprising gulf between nations on attitudes to
truth, and why there is a growing gap between Muslims
and the Christian or lay population in some western
countries.*

5. Some influences on behaviour   43

*This chapter considers how nations regard rules and
regulations, and why some countries love orderliness,
while others seem to have no sense of discipline. It
explores the leadership styles of East and West, as well
as attitudes to risk-taking, privacy, individuality and
achievement.*

6. The five stages of cultural learning   57

*How do you fit in if you are a foreigner? And how do you
enable foreigners to fit in with you? The virtuous and
vicious spirals of fitting in provide the guide, leading on
to the five stages of learning which will give you the
insight and mindset that you need.*

7. When is a 'Yes' not a 'Yes'   67

*Ever been driven to distraction by the unreliability of
people from abroad? Find out why Indians say 'Yes'
when they want to say 'No', but don't know how, and
why some people just cannot say 'That's too expensive'.
Could it be about saving face...?*

8. Making English international   76

*Because English is so widely used, especially in
business, it is tempting to believe that everyone can
understand it. It isn't so, and direct translations can
often leave the real meaning behind. Find out what it
means when the Spanish or Mexicans say 'Mañana'.
This chapter provides practical guidance on bridging the
communication gap.*

9. **Connecting with the audience** 88
   It is always important to meet your listeners'
   expectations when speaking in public. But when your
   audience is foreign, you may find their listening habits
   disconcerting! Every nation listens differently, and you
   may have to take into account how they were taught to
   learn, what grabs their attention, and what can turn off
   an audience in that particular country.

10. **International presentations** 104
    The content and structure of a presentation should
    always be adapted to the tastes of the nation receiving it,
    even if the presentation is in English. This chapter
    illustrates how to avoid cultural clashes, and how to
    match the rhythm and pace of an international
    audience, while retaining the merits of the Anglo-Saxon
    approach to business presentations.

11. **Tips on communicating with different nations** 113
    Concluding Part 1, this chapter consists of quick
    reference bullet points on how to communicate with a
    number of European nations plus Japan and the US,
    and how to conduct yourself in international meetings. It
    is not an attempt to provide all the international
    protocols, but gives a very useful spread to guide your
    communications even with countries not listed here.

PART 2 Quick Reference Guide for Busy People 129

12. **The Seven relationship danger points of business** 131
    This chapter focuses on seven areas in which significant
    communication takes place, any of which can undermine
    the relationships you may be trying to develop. It covers
    international meetings and negotiations, contracts,
    cross-cultural management and selling, political
    correctness and 'greasing the wheels'.

13. **The ten best tips for doing business around the world**   **161**
*This is a reference section to help you understand and
deal with business contacts in most of the major nations.
It includes attitudes to rules, management and
communication styles, and much else besides, including
public holidays and feast days. It is a quick dip, either to
refresh your memory or to provide a prompt for further
research.*

14. **Corruption index**   **239**
*How honest is any nation? This table provides a notional
guide to each country's propensity to be influenced by
personal gain.*

Index   **243**

About the Authors

Deborah Swallow is a professional speaker on business issues, from the viewpoint of an entrepreneur, and the author of *Culture Shock Finland*. She reshaped the fortunes of her family business, turning it around with a proactive policy of acquisition and diversification. Along the way, she combined the traditional roles of housewife and mother with those of a businesswoman, gaining a string of qualifications and several active directorships. In 1999 she won the **UK National Training Award** in her own right, and went on to co-found **4C International Limited**, a training company specialising in cross-cultural communication.

She speaks French and Spanish, and once worked as an interpreter. Her work in cross-culture began when she was invited to conduct internationalisation courses for small businesses in Scandinavia, guiding them in doing business across national borders. Through 4C International Ltd she has trained diplomats and senior business executives in Europe, Africa and the Middle East.

She believes passionately that a business brings wealth to the society in which it operates, and that the leaders of that business can contribute to the spiritual wealth of the world by improving our understanding of other cultures. She believes that businesses which establish themselves in other countries should contribute to the development and advancement of those countries in social as well as economic ways.

In writing this book, Deborah hopes to leave the reader with a sense of wonder at the diversity of nations, and a sympathetic understanding of their values. She hopes this book will engender respect for difference as well as a willingness to communicate with harmony.

The training programmes she has helped to develop through 4C International Ltd are all designed to promote international understanding. The company's name itself stands for Cross-cultural Communication Consultants, and she not only provides guidance on communication techniques, but helps to refocus the thinking of her course delegates, so that they step away from 'the way we do things in our country' and find a way to form a two-way bridge with their counterparts from other cultures.

Phillip Khan-Panni is a professional speaker and the author of four other books on communication skills. He has also been running training programmes through his own consultancies, *Speaking & Presentation Skills* and *PKP Communicators* since the early 1990s.

He has probably won more public speaking contests than anyone in Europe, including the UK championship seven times, the Anglo-Irish championship three times, and the Silver Medal in the World Championship of Public Speaking, held in San Diego, California.

He can not only perform as a highly effective speaker, but is the man who can teach any business person to make a decent speech or presentation. One airline executive said, 'Never speak in public without first speaking to Phillip.' His books are written with the same verve as he puts into his speeches. One reviewer said that he 'writes with power and passion about putting power and passion into your public speaking and presentations. The ideas teem, the pace is fast and, above all, the writer has been there, got it wrong, worked out why and moved on.'

One thing he got right was the management of sales teams. With one team that he took over, he tripled the revenue in his first year, and was the most successful classified advertisement manager in the history of the *Daily Express.*

An outstanding wordsmith, with a business background in advertising, newspaper publishing and direct marketing, he was senior copywriter at *Reader's Digest* for eight years, and ran his own direct marketing creative agency for four years until a family tragedy cut it short.

As co-founder of **4C International Ltd**, he coaches senior business executives and diplomats in communication skills, both written and spoken. The techniques he teaches are effective and easy to apply. More importantly, he imparts a new understanding of the communication process and inspires people to want to do it better. This book captures much of his flair and enthusiasm, with narratives that flow from his own multi-cultural experiences. In many ways it's a personal declaration.

www.4CInternational.com

Preface

'Let my house not be walled on four sides,
Let all the windows be open,
Let all the cultures blow in,

But let no culture blow me off my feet.'
(Mahatma Gandhi)

Clairol had a new product for the German market. It was a curling iron and their advisers coined the name 'Mist Stick'. It flopped. Clairol apparently did not know that 'mist' is German slang for dung. Not many Germans felt the need for a dung stick.

Then there was the celebrated case of the Scandinavian company, Electrolux, who promoted their vacuum cleaners in America with the slogan: 'Nothing sucks like an Electrolux'.

Pepsi decided to break into the Chinese market with a direct translation of their slogan, 'Come alive with the Pepsi Generation'. It translated into Chinese as: 'Pepsi brings your ancestors back from the grave'.

These simple mistakes cost their companies a great deal of money and caused immense embarrassment. Our own mistakes in dealing with people from other cultures may not cost us dearly, but they can matter just as much. For it is a fact that the world has altered dramatically in the past few years, and the pace of change is accelerating. Like it or not, we have to deal with people whose styles and expectations are very different from our own, whether for business or pleasure. International travel is a normal part of our lives, and we do business with people in or from other countries.

How successful we are depends on how well we connect as individuals. It's the people in your company, or it's you as an individual, who must make the contacts and commitments, it's the human exchanges that make all the difference. For those exchanges to work well, you must understand how people from other cultures think and operate. You need to know how to communicate with them, by phone, email, letter or in person. Because of globalisation and the influence of television, people all over the world dress the same, seem the same, but they are not the same. Their history, heritage, language, geography and customs – their culture – make them different. Hence the need for cross-cultural understanding. Hence this book.

Imagine being faced with the prospect of entertaining a business associate from another country in your home for a few days. Or going to stay with his family abroad. Imagine the questions that would flood into your mind: how to address him. . . what to feed him. . . how will he feed you. . . will he take his shoes off when he enters your home. . . should you take your shoes off in his home. . . should you take flowers or chocolates, when invited out for dinner. . . does he have a sense of humour. . . does he prefer a bath or a shower. . . what time does he start work in the morning. . .? Now imagine being sent to a foreign country to drum up some business for your company. Do they accept cold calls on the phone. . . do you need to write to make an appointment. . . should you call them by their first names. . . how do they say 'Mister' or 'Madam' or 'please' and 'thank you'. Do they ever say 'Yes' at a first meeting... what are their protocols...?

Doing business in another country is much more than flying out, staying in a posh hotel and eating different food. It's entering a different world, and you need to learn the rules. For that you need patience, preparation, an open mind – and this book.

All business travellers need to know something about the country they are visiting, its people and its customs. They also need an appreciation of the differences that visitors bring with them. And that's not all. Businesses need to realise that cultural differences exist on their doorstep. They almost certainly have cultural diversity among their staff and their clients or customers. Are they sensitive to that diversity, and do they have a cross-cultural understanding?

A person's culture is a bit like an iceberg, with only about 10 per cent visible. The remaining 90 per cent remains unknown until we get to know that person. Meanwhile, we are apt to leap to judgements based on stereotypes and generalisations. That can lead us to wrong conclusions and inappropriate behaviour. And when there is a conflict of any kind, we can only resolve it if we tune in to the other person and press the right buttons.

Some cultures are individualistic, others are communitarian. Some are assertive, others are passive. There isn't one right approach to any of them. What you need is a sensitivity and a willingness to learn what works. The starting place is an understanding of how different cultures operate, and that's what this book aims to provide.

Today's international companies, whatever their size, cannot afford to ignore the high rate of failure among expatriates, and the resulting high costs. The failure rate can be as high as 25-33 per cent. There is the direct cost of relocating and setting up the executive and his or her family. And there is the indirect cost of repatriating the failed executive and recapturing his or her skills, which may have been damaged along with the loss of self-confidence.

There is a whole raft of new skills to be learned when an executive is transferred abroad, and not every employer pays enough attention to providing the necessary training. This book may not, on its own, redress the balance, but it will help in creating awareness of what is needed, and provide many of the answers. It will go a long way towards creating the right mindset for effective cross-cultural dealings and communication.

Our approach goes a long way beyond language, although direct translations provide much hilarity. One English speaker in Russia used the expression, 'Out of sight, out of mind.' The Russians translated this literally, without understanding the meaning of the saying, and it came out as 'Blind idiot'. To limit ourselves to mere linguistic differences would indeed be to operate as blind idiots! Instead, we have tried to explain how cultural differences cause us to communicate with different stride patterns, and even to march in totally different directions. Our purpose is to help the reader to become sensitive to those differences and develop a respect for the way people from other cultures communicate.

Our company, 4C International Limited, provides a number of training programmes and one-to-one coaching in cross cultural communication skills, both written and spoken, and they would complete the job begun by this book.

Deborah Swallow and Phillip Khan-Panni

Part 1
Bridging the
Communication Gap

1

Why This Book

'The trouble with this world is not that people know too little, but that they know too much that ain't so.'
(Mark Twain, *The Innocents Abroad*)

Florida, said the travel agent, is full of retired English folk. Yet Deborah, on a recent visit there, spoke Spanish more often than she spoke English. Swathes of America are more Hispanic than Anglo, and some Californian businesses put a Spanish message on their telephone answering machines before the English version, in the expectation that most callers will be speakers of Spanish, not English. It causes friction between the communities.

English may be the language of business in many parts of the world, but it isn't the only one. Research indicates that by the year 2020 there will be three principal languages around the world: English, Spanish and Chinese. English speakers will be faced with the twin problems of having to learn how to speak one of those languages, and coping with the cultural differences that accompany them. This book will help. Although aimed primarily at English speakers, it will be equally useful to anyone whose own language is not English, but who has to do business in that language.

CROSS CULTURAL SENSITIVITY GIVES YOU THE EDGE

In the past, when foreigners were a novelty, it was forgivable to make mistakes in dealing with them. These days, however, cross-border travel is commonplace, and we know so much more about other countries. We are therefore expected to understand how our counterparts in other countries think and behave. It is no longer acceptable to demand that they fit in with us. In an increasingly competitive business world, those who understand different cultures will have the edge.

Cultural diversity is everywhere, and not only across borders. It is important to understand how to cope with cultural diversity among your staff and your customers on the doorstep. If companies conducted proper exit interviews with all the key staff who leave unexpectedly, and all the customers who turn to a competitor, they would be horrified to learn that insensitive handling by their own people was one of the prime causes. Stand in a bank or building society, or at the check-in desk of any airline, and listen to how 'foreign' customers are treated. Loiter in the reception areas of large solicitors or insurance companies in the City of London, and watch for the level of courtesy shown to visitors from abroad.

Listen to the TV and radio interviews with sporting stars from other countries, and marvel at the interviewers' use of metaphors, clichés and colloquialisms. An African marathon runner may fall across the line in the London Marathon, only to have a microphone stuck in his face, with simple-sounding but baffling questions like, 'Did you feel you were doing fine when you started to open up?'

What's 'doing fine' and 'open up' to someone who doesn't speak much English?

IS THIS KIND OF IGNORANCE BLISS?

We have encountered countless stories of amazing ignorance, not all of them apocryphal. A Croatian diplomat of our acquaintance was visiting Vienna, when she met an American tourist who asked where she came from. 'I come from Croatia,' she replied. The American then asked, 'When you came here, to Vienna, was it a civilisation shock for you?' Being a diplomat, our friend refrained from mentioning that Croatia has a 1400-year history which has included connections with Hungary, Turkey and Napoleon's France, and cultural traditions that would shame her questioner.

Phillip grew up in India, which is one of the world's few nuclear powers, as we are reminded every time the conflict with Pakistan erupts over Kashmir. Soon after arriving to live in Britain he was asked, 'Do they have electricity in India?'

Questions like these indicate a deep-rooted ignorance of other nations. It means that it will be difficult for such people to find a basis for comparison. Inevitably there will be problems of communication. It's hard to make proper contact if you don't understand how the other person lives and thinks, if you have no idea of the kind of society that exists in the other person's country, if you think you are speaking to a backward person when that person may actually be better educated than you, and used to a higher standard of living. It works in reverse too.

A visitor to London from the Philippines was being driven through one of the downmarket areas, and she was told, 'This is a slum area.' She looked at the shabby brick buildings around her, contrasted them with the shanties of Philippine slums, and asked, 'How can you tell it's a slum?' A London slum is a world apart from a slum in Manila.

HELPING YOU TO COPE WITH DIFFERENCES

These examples are by no means isolated exceptions. Even in the business world, such misconceptions are widespread. Global village? Not yet. But we are getting there, and this book aims to make a contribution to better understanding between people from different cultures. It will guide your understanding of how people communicate, how that differs from nation to nation, and how to understand what is going on in the minds of your listeners, whether in the formal context when, for example, you are making presentations to a seated audience, or when dealing one to one, face to face.

Communication across cultures is poorly done. The evidence is all around us. If we get it wrong, the consequences can be disastrous. Yet, if we get it right, the opportunities are great.

This book's purpose is to help you to communicate more effectively with non-native English speakers, mainly in business but also in daily life. We'll do that by identifying some typical misconceptions (and some that are not so obvious) and suggesting ways to avoid or overcome them. Even more importantly, we want to help you to understand how your communication is received and processed by those with cultural backgrounds that differ from your own.

This book will show you how to improve your communication skills. That does not mean limiting yourself to polishing up how you prepare and deliver a speech or presentation. It means taking account of what goes on in the minds and hearts of your hearers. The way people listen and process information is influenced by such powerful factors as:

- The way they think.
- Their value sets.
- The way they make decisions.
- How they do business.
- Their reasoning processes.
- Their cultural traditions.

CULTURAL DIVERSITY ON YOUR DOORSTEP

Now, cultural differences aren't only 'out there' – abroad. They exist right on your doorstep. Already 7 per cent of Britons are non-white, and you can add to that figure the whites of foreign descent. Britain is a multicultural society, and so are many countries of the world. All large companies, and most smaller ones, have multicultural staff. Probably every company has multicultural customers or clients as well. To ignore those differences is to risk losing key staff and those who spend money with your company.

In a suburban branch of a major bank, we saw an Indian shopkeeper come in and ask to see the manager. The bank had an open-plan layout with a couple of tables and chairs positioned near the queue of customers. After a while a young man, clearly too junior to be the bank manager, came out into the open area and invited the shopkeeper to sit at one of the tables and discuss his business – in the hearing of all the customers in the queue. The shopkeeper looked very uncomfortable, and quickly left after asking a couple of unimportant questions. We would not have been surprised if he had changed banks after that incident. It was a blatant example of cultural insensitivity, and was received by the Indian as an insult.

In twenty-first century Britain, many taboos have been broken, and there is much less inclination to protect privacy. There is less shame and not much embarrass-ment. People blush less. It's an open society in which people discuss their earnings and their sex lives without qualms... and they probably expect that the same standards apply to everyone. They do not. They especially do not apply to communities of people who originated in the East, for whom respect is a key word – respect for elders, for personal privacy, for personal status, for 'face'.

We hope to provide the insights to build bridges between East and West, between old and new, and to communicate with harmony.

2

Why Speaking Louder and Slower Doesn't Work

All good people agree,
And all good people say,
All nice people, like us, are We
And everyone else is They.
But if you cross over the sea
Instead of over the way,
You may end up by (think of it!)
Looking on We
As only a sort of They.
          (Rudyard Kipling, *We and They*)

Phillip presented his Oriental face at the garage where his car had just been serviced. The man at the counter asked, 'How would you like to pay?' Jokingly, Phillip replied, 'Slowly!' The man then said, 'How...would...you...like...to...pay?' Generations of Englishmen have adopted the speak-louder-and-slower approach to addressing foreigners. Clearly, that kind of thinking is alive and well. But it doesn't work, and nor should it.

Consider this: have you ever found yourself unconsciously matching the speaking style of the person you were speaking to? For example, if you were speaking to a foreigner whose English was a bit hesitant, did you find yourself speaking less fluently than usual, perhaps even ungrammatically? And have you never adopted the accent of the other person...perhaps an American accent, or cockney or north country? Such adaptability is instinctive and entirely natural. It flows from a desire to communicate, and to find common ground. It is one of the keys to cross-cultural communication. We instinctively sense that if we make sounds that are similar to those made by the other person, we will be understood more readily.

And yet, the reality is that we do not all communicate the same way. When we speak in English to foreigners, we look for those tiny signs of understanding, the brightness of the eyes, the almost imperceptible nods of agreement, the grunts that signify that they are following what we are saying. When those signs are absent, we assume that our words are not being understood, and we try harder. We speak louder and slower.

WE ALL PROCESS INFORMATION DIFFERENTLY

However, the foreigner may have understood your words perfectly well. His blank look may be because he is weighing up the credibility of your message, or wondering why you are expressing the message so differently from the way he might have put it himself. It may be that he is considering whether he agrees with you, and that he does not consider it appropriate to show a response until he has decided where he stands. Freya Stark, in *The Journey's Echo*, wrote: 'Every country has its way of saying things. The importance is that which lies behind people's words.' To understand what lies behind the words of someone from another culture, you need cultural adaptability.

In some eastern cultures it is unsophisticated to show surprise. Someone raised that way will respond very coolly to dramatic news, let alone ordinary conversation. A westerner may well imagine that he is not getting through, or that the easterner has not understood. He is used to his listeners responding with 'Really?' and 'Oh ah!' and nods of agreement throughout the exchange, and he is put out when his oriental listener merely nods at the end to indicate, 'Message received and understood'.

We all process information differently, and the way we do so is reflected in the language we use. However, it is important to remember which came first, the mental processes or the language. Clearly, language followed the mental processes. Or rather, the way a nation uses its language indicates how its people think. The English language, for example, can be used in more ways than one. Brits and Americans use the active voice, direct speech and action verbs. The people of Malawi tend to speak and write in the passive voice, third person, and indirect speech. The Arabs have a similar approach. Same language, different attitudes.

In communicating with other cultures, cultural adaptability is more important than language skills. You need a strong willingness to understand what it is that causes the people of another culture to think and behave the way they do. You need to 'tune in'. Cultural adaptability is about switching your communication style to facilitate understanding or to make it easier to work together. You may need to accept that other cultures need time to consider what you say before agreeing or accepting. It may strike you as resistance or even discourtesy, but it may only be the normal response in their culture. Speaking louder and slower will only make things worse.

TRAPS FOR THE UNWARY

It can be baffling to hear some British broadcasters, and the way they mangle their own language. Here are a few gems:

'They're known by their Christian names in Turkey.' (John Motson, BBC TV Football)

'Not only has the pace been constant, it's been increasing.' (Brendan Foster, BBC TV Athletics)

'That's inches away from being millimetre perfect.' (Ted Lowe, BBC TV Snooker)

'He went down like a sack of potatoes and made a meal of it.' (Trevor Brooking)

'You can't compare Lennox Lewis to Muhammad Ali. But he's not dissimilar.' (Gary Mason)

'People started calling me "Fiery" because "Fiery" rhymes with Fred, just as "Typhoon" rhymes with Tyson. (Fred Trueman)

'The French are not normally a Nordic skiing nation.' (Ron Pickering, BBC TV Skiing)

'Now the boot is on the other Schumacher.' (Murray Walker)

'They came through absolutely together with Alan Wells in first place.' (David Coleman)

Some of these examples are mixed metaphors, and brings to mind the way we use language. Colloquial English is full of metaphors, similes and non-literal speech. The English themselves tend to use circumlocution, understatement and irony, all of which can be confusing for a non-native speaker of English. 'Not bad' in England is a term of praise. 'Rather pleased' is a declaration of great happiness. 'Not unadjacent to...' is a contemporary expression meaning 'very nearly'. Often, when expressing more than one idea in the same sentence, the speaker will use (and mangle) two or more metaphors, just as Trevor Brooking and Murray Walker did in the examples above. In a later chapter we shall consider in greater detail how the English language is used to convey shades of meaning, and how that might be simplified and slowed down to help your listeners to understand and follow what is being said.

TEN KEYS TO EFFECTIVE CROSS-CULTURAL COMMUNICATION

Right now, let's consider ten essential elements that form the right approach to communicating with people whose own language patterns are very different from your own, and whose command of your language is formal rather than colloquial. For effective cross-cultural communication, a person needs to:

1. acknowledge own assumptions, i.e. what drives his or her attitudes

2. recognise 'invisible' differences that exist

3. welcome change

4. consider alternatives

5. avoid generalisations

6. respect the individual

7. be patient and tolerant

8. be sensitive to non-verbal cues

9. remember 'face'

10. listen.

Own assumptions

Are you an action-oriented communicator? Do you expect your listeners to understand-agree-act? Do you expect them to signal that they are doing so? Be aware that people from some countries (a) do not communicate that way, and (b) might dislike being expected to respond like that. Think about how you'd react to an untalented comedian (or an acquaintance who cannot tell a joke) digging you in the ribs all evening and expecting you to laugh at a succession of execrable stories or jokes. That's why we should avoid imposing our expectations on others, and listen/watch for *their* way of responding.

Invisible differences

Good manners may prevent others from letting you know when you have transgressed, so it's not always easy to recognise when you are on the wrong track. A good approach is to adopt an attitude of wanting to learn about another person's cultural expectations, and *ask*. For example, if you are having a meal together and you are served something that could be eaten with the fingers, ask what is normal in the other person's country. Always be sensitive to 'seniority', which could be based on age, status or gender, and observe basic courtesy, such as not interrupting when they are in mid sentence. Equally, be prepared to accept their deference if you are the senior person.

Welcome change

You need to be prepared to set aside your habitual way of doing or saying things, and look for the advantages of emulating the style of the other person. Perhaps he talks with his hands – does that add meaning to what he is saying? Perhaps he doesn't say 'please' or 'thank you' as often as you do – but is that rudeness on his part, or is he demonstrating that he feels comfortable and familiar with you, as a member of your family might do?

Consider alternatives

The communication process involves much more than language alone. In the give and take of a dialogue, there are expectations on both sides, some of which are met, others not. For example, it may be your style to settle things over the telephone, but the other person may be used to agreeing things in writing. You may be used to making decisions unilaterally, whereas he may be a committee man. When judo was introduced into Britain, initially it awarded only white belts (for novices) and black belts (for masters). However, the British required intermediate grades to mark their progress, so other coloured belts were introduced. The question to ask yourself is, 'What will get the result I want?' Be pragmatic and do what works.

Stereotypes and generalisations

There is an old saying that the moment an Englishman

opens his mouth he is immediately condemned by another. This is because accent and vocabulary betray the speaker's class, and the English are deeply class conscious. They are equally quick to judge foreigners according to the stereotypes and caricatures of common mythology. Unfortunately that simply raises barriers to proper communication. In a lighthearted paradox, Phillip tends to say, 'As a rule I never generalise' (itself a generalisation), but that leaves the non-English scratching their heads.

Respect and the individual

If your objective is to connect with the other person and communicate well with him, it would be useful to think of him as an individual, not as a representative of his company or his country. The key word is *respect*. Build a relationship based on that.

Patience and tolerance

First impressions linger forever. A person whose first language is not the same as yours may have difficulty in understanding what you are saying, and that may make them seem slow. The way you handle that will colour your relationship for all time. Remember that everyone has something to offer, and those from a different culture can help you to refine your communication skills.

Non-verbal cues

Each nation has its own communication style. The British consider it impolite to interrupt, while the Latins interrupt all the time. In contrast, Orientals pause before responding, not because they have reservations about what has been said but because they wish to consider it properly. Similarly, vocal tone and volume should be adjusted to suit the norms of the people you are talking to. Also, you should look for signs of discomfort (such as turning the body away from you) and 'project' less when that happens. Pay particular attention to the way in which an Oriental says 'Yes' – they find it hard to say 'No' and will often say 'Yes' even when it is hard for them to deliver. Avoid eye contact in the Far East, and do not reach out to help an Arab lady out of the car.

'Face'

This is one of the least understood concepts. In simple terms, you should always avoid making the other person feel uncomfortable, especially in front of others. Sometimes, 'face' is affected as a knock-on consequence of your decision to alter your status. In a hierarchical society, if you are the boss you are expected to have certain symbols of your status, such as a posh car, because everyone below your rank would have to have something less. If you choose to have a modest car, for example, you would cause your subordinates to lose face by having even more modest cars. Causing someone to lose face is the ultimate insult. The Japanese, for example, cannot understand colloquial English spoken at normal pace, and may therefore indulge in elaborate responses to save face – but you will not get the result you may have been expecting.

Listen

Hearing is not the same as listening. You need to listen, not only for what is being said, but for what lies behind what is being said. Listen for the clues in the speech pattern, in particular for how direct the other person is. Some people freely criticise ideas, in the belief that they are not attacking the individual personally. Others take all criticisms personally. Some cultures (e.g. northern European) communicate the salient facts. Others (e.g. Italian) value the process of communication more as a means of connecting the emotions, confirming status and reinforcing relationships. Others (e.g. Japanese) seek to promote harmony. What can you hear?

DIFFERENCES CAN GET IN THE WAY

Differences in communication styles can be irritating, and that can undermine trust. Phillip found an excellent dentist who did a first rate job when one of his crowns fell out just before an important training assignment. The dentist was newly arrived in Britain from Sweden, and used some impressively advanced techniques. But later, when she was discussing a more extensive programme of treatment to rectify poor dentistry that has been done in the past, her limited command of English began to get in the way. This is the sequence of what happened behind the spoken words:

1. What she proposed sounded good – at first.
2. However, her detailed explanations were hard to understand.
3. Phillip had to ask three times for clarification.
4. Doubts began to enter his mind.
5. In his mind he started to question her logic.
6. He became uncertain of her engineering skills.
7. He wondered if she would leave him with an unsightly smile.

8. He started looking for a way out.

...and all because her limited English reduced the credibility of her proposals.

It goes beyond language. Many a business disaster has resulted from trying to transplant a product or idea from one country to another without taking account of cultural or lifestyle differences.

◆ **IKEA's** entry into the American market was disastrous. The Swedish beds were too narrow; they didn't sell matching bedroom furniture; their kitchen cupboards were too narrow to hold pizza-size dinner plates; drinking glasses were too small to hold all the ice that Americans like.

◆ **Coca-Cola** had a disaster with its 2 litre bottles in Spain – the fridges weren't big enough to hold them. The Spanish like to have their drinks in the fridge.

◆ The launch of **UK cake mixes** in Japan flopped totally. Market testing showed that the Japanese loved the cakes but sales of the cake mixes were zero. Why? The Japanese don't have ovens, which is a prerequisite for cooking sponges.

INTERNATIONAL DIFFERENCES IN WORK RELATED VALUES

Few joint ventures work and last. Many seem like marriages made in heaven but after a few months cultural clashes erode the potentially lucrative relationship. Most fall apart because of differences in approach to power and authority, time, communication style, and formality.

Consider American firms joining with Mexican ones. The Americans become frustrated by the slowness of Mexican decision-making. Mexico is a hierarchical culture and only the very senior managers make decisions, which means long delays as each decision awaits its turn in the backlog on each senior person's desk. Respect and loyalty to these managers is a high priority in Mexico, so workers would never try to get above themselves and try to usurp the authority of their bosses.

Also, Mexicans have a very relaxed approach to time. In their view, Americans are always trying to push things through too fast. Americans, for their part, consider the Mexicans idle. Communication between the two groups is difficult, not because of language, but because of style and attitude. Americans are very direct and seemingly rude and disrespectful. Mexicans are indirect, and their politeness can be seen as a way to hide problems and errors.

Worst of all, Mexicans are very macho and have huge egos. They can't accept losing face or self-esteem. Their conflicts with the Americans are not about facts (which are quite easy to resolve), but about style and tone (which are not).

Americans are have-a-go heroes who are prepared to take the plunge and make corrections as they go along. They hate the Brits' ponderous, methodological manner of planning and covering all contingencies. The American company, Microsoft, puts out software that isn't fully developed. They wait for users to find bugs in the system. The Germans, on the other hand, would want it to be perfect before releasing a product.

Cross-cultural communication is about understanding how people from other cultures process information, and what they expect from formal exchanges, especially at the start of a relationship. Speaking slower and louder is no longer acceptable as the right way to get through to Johnny Foreigner.

3

East is East and West is West

*'Oh, East is East, and West is West, and never
the Twain shall meet'*
(Rudyard Kipling)

Of course the twain do meet in today's small world – but
research since the 1980s has illuminated huge differences
between Confucian thinking in the Chinese cultural area,
western thinking in general, and the Muslim-based
thinking of middle Asia.

The suicide bombings of Al Qaeda and the Palestinians
have baffled westerners. Yet the tensions in the Middle
East have heightened the West's awareness of the Muslim
world and the difference in thinking there. The burgeon-
ing economies of the Arab world have attracted
increasing numbers of westerners to holiday and even
work in places that were once obscure names on the
neglected pages of the world atlas. The area around
central London's Marble Arch has acquired an Arab
look, with many a shop sign in the curly right-to-left
Arabic script, and late night café customers sit at
pavement tables with their hubble bubble hookahs. East
and West are meeting more frequently.

As recently as the late 1960s, the poet-writer, Dom
Moraes, revisited India, the land of his birth, and found

that he was a stranger. Speaking no word of any Indian language, he was in the hands of his manservant, and had to learn how to manage the master-servant relationship. He learned, also, that he could not bypass his man and deal directly with lower caste subcontractors, such as the sweeper, and that the hierarchy had to be maintained. He learned, but did not understand, that his man would fiercely protect him from exploitation by vendors, but considered it his right to swindle his master on the daily food shopping. He noticed that servants would not make eye contact with their masters, nor do any of the things that build a personal relationship. In short, he became acutely aware that East is East and very different from the West.

Of course, the East has long been part of the British scene, with curry now the most popular dish in restaurants and take-aways. Yet, amazingly for a nation that only recently relinquished a vast empire, and which has adopted a sizeable number of Indian words into the language, Britain remains largely ignorant of eastern ways. In London, the Sikhs in Southall, the Bengalis in Brick Lane and the Hindus in Harrow have clustered together like the Arabs of Marble Arch, in a sort of reverse colonisation, forming communities that are distinct from the host community.

It provides the host community with an opportunity to learn about diverse cultures, but it's one that few have taken advantage of. Perhaps the Brits are not very curious. When the Indian cricketers were playing in England, we were talking to a young cricket fan about the bowling action of Anil Kumble, India's leading leg spinner. Most of the time he delivers a ball that lands and changes direction from right to left. But occasionally he delivers one that travels the other way. He calls it his '*Doosra*'. Our young friend knew about it, knew the term, but although he had a large number of Indian friends, he didn't know that '*Doosra*' means 'other'. He had never asked.

Unfortunately, host communities often feel threatened by visible gatherings of foreigners whose customs, dress and language are different from their own. They feel anxious about losing their jobs, their homes and even their womenfolk to the invaders. Yet not every society is antagonistic towards newcomers. The Japanese have a concept they call *kyosei,* which means living and working together for the common good – enabling cooperation and mutual prosperity to coexist with healthy and fair competition.

Let's identify the main points of difference between East and West. They are:

- attitude to time
- focus on objective
- respect
- seniority
- politeness
- personal space
- hospitality
- importance of family
- individual or community.

IT TAKES AS LONG AS IT TAKES

In southern Europe and many eastern countries, deadlines

are considered to be loose indicators, not commitments. When Debbie first went to live in Spain, she believed (as much of the English-speaking world probably does) that the word *mañana* meant 'tomorrow'. Consequently, she was often frustrated when she turned up the following day to collect whatever had been promised, only to be sent away again empty handed. In time she realised that, for the Spanish, *mañana* simply means 'not today'.

An equally frustrating word, regularly used in the Middle East, is *N'sha'llah* or *Inshallah*. It translates as 'God willing' but actually means, 'I take no responsibility for what might happen in the future'. Both the Spanish and the Arabs (and the nations in between) have a relaxed attitude to time keeping and deadlines, and things get done when they get around to them. One Sri Lankan who lives and works in an Arab country has a cynical view of *Inshallah*. He says, 'When someone says 'God willing' I take it to mean 'I'm not willing'.'

Early in her Spanish period, Deborah invited her boss and his wife for dinner at her apartment. Eight o'clock (the usual dinner party hour in Britain) came and went, but no sign of her guests. At nine o'clock she decided not to waste the food she had prepared, so she knocked on the doors of her neighbours, and invited them in. They were just finishing dinner at 10.30 pm when her boss and his wife arrived, two and a half hours late. That is to say, they were late by Deborah's reckoning, but not by their own norms.

Michael Tipper, the World Memory Silver Medallist, was conducting his first training course in the Middle East. He gave them a break and asked them to return in 15 minutes. Some 40 minutes later they drifted back. Not only did that disrupt Michael's schedule, but the day's impetus and rhythm were lost. They did not notice.

When we conducted our first training programme in southern Africa, the delegates were never on time, and the total numbers varied day by day, from 12 to 16. One delegate even stated that he had thought of coming along just for one day, to find out if the course was interesting, and had decided to stay. They were being sponsored at great cost by a European government, but that made little impression on them. Their values were different from ours.

It works in reverse too. Certain western practices can give offence to easterners or cause disharmony. It is well known that you should not show the soles of your shoes to an Oriental, yet many a person will rest the ankle of one leg on the knee of the other, with the sole of his shoe directed at the person sitting opposite. On trains in England, it is a common practice for people to put their feet on the seats opposite, causing Orientals (and some westerners) to recoil in horror and distaste.

Certain practices give offence simply because they are insensitive, and some nations are more likely to take offence than others. However, two thoughts should guide us:

1. We all react when someone does commonplace things differently from us, whether it be a handshake or the way they eat a steak. We therefore need to be aware of the reflex of prejudice that is within us.

2. We need to be sensitive towards others, and aware of our own conduct, in case it gives offence to them.

Above all, we should never cause someone to lose face. Not only is it discourteous, it can make an enemy for life. Face is a concept that dominates social and business contact throughout the Far East, not just in China and Japan. The Indonesians have a term, *Malu*, to describe causing someone to lose face or status. Indians may call it something else, but they are just as conscious of saving face. Even the Italians are face conscious. In films about the Mafia, you will hear the Dons say, 'He didn't show me no respect.' By that they mean, 'He caused me to lose face.' The Dons' solution would be to terminate the offending individual. Oriental business contacts may not go to such extremes, but they might terminate the relationship all the same.

Losing face is to lose dignity, and for the Chinese that is like losing their eyes, nose and mouth. The embarrassment is actually felt in the face. Social relations should be conducted in such a way that everybody's face is maintained. Paying respect to someone is called 'giving face'. Think of the English expression, 'I couldn't show my face in there' – it refers to the way we experience humiliation, and goes a long way towards helping westerners to understand the concept of face saving.

Let's now take a look at some of the ways in which East and West think and function differently.

Meetings

Whether formal or informal, a business meeting with a prospective customer or client for most westerners (especially Americans) is supposed to result in an outcome. They want agreement, and will consider themselves successful or not according to whether they obtained agreement. However, eastern and southern nations treat such meetings as opportunities to develop the relationship, so that they can later decide if they want to do business with the other party.

Time keeping

If you issue an invitation for dinner in different countries, you will have totally different experiences. Suppose your invitation is for 7.00 pm. This is when you might expect your guests to arrive in different countries:

Germany	7.00
US Midwest	6.55
Japan	6.00
UK	7.15
Norway	7.00 – 7.15
Italy	8.00
Greece	8.00 – 10.00
Spain	10.30
India	8.00 – 9.00

Of course these timings are not absolute, nor do they always apply in those countries, but they indicate a typical approach to timekeeping. With Germans being precisely on time, the Brits politely arriving a few minutes late to allow the hostess to be properly ready to receive, and the

Indians operating on what they themselves call 'Indian Standard Time'.

Agreements

The westerner, and especially the northern European, expects an agreement to be honoured, and takes a dim view of any deviation from it. Easterners are more flexible and tolerant. This is due to a difference in their expectations. The western view is that an agreement is as absolute as it can be, imposing a duty on both parties to deliver, or negotiate an acceptable variation. Easterners regard agreements as expressions of a willingness to try. If circumstances change, making it difficult or impossible to deliver, they may not even try, because the cosmic forces that brought about the change are greater than the expectations of the other party to the agreement.

Humour

Many westerners (and probably all Americans) seem to believe that speeches and presentations need the launch pad of humour. Yet there are some nations that dislike and look down on attempts to make a business audience laugh. With such audiences, if you open with a joke you will close their minds. They will take it as an insult. Japanese audiences expect you to treat them with respect, even telling them why you respect them so much. An opening apology is much more acceptable.

These are just a few of the more obvious areas of difference. They and others will be developed later in the book.

$$\boxed{4}$$

East/West Influences on Thinking

'What I say is this (the Indian man remarked)
and this I do not say to all Englishmen:
    God made us different, you and I, and your
    fathers and my fathers. For one thing, we
    have not the same notions of honesty and
    speaking the truth. That is not our fault,
    because we are made so. And look now what
    you do? You come and judge us by your own
    standards of morality. You are, of course,
    too hard on us. And again I tell you, you are
    great fools in this matter. Who are we to
    have your morals, or you to have ours?'
                  (Rudyard Kipling, *East and West*)

DIFFERENT ATTITUDES, NOT WRONG ATTITUDES
There are a number of standard influences on thinking and attitudes, which occur in all societies. Three, in particular, are universal:

1. Respectful: juniors to seniors.
2. Collaborative: towards the group or society.
3. Gender-based.

It is human nature to want to assert our own point of view and get it accepted, so we need to understand how those three attitudes influence the outcome of our communication. This chapter explores some of the ways in which East and West think differently, and the traditional influences that have led to these styles of thinking and being.

In a balanced society, the young are taught respect, and they carry that into their working lives. Sometimes it is necessary to wield the threat of dismissal to remind them of the need to be respectful, but modern laws to protect employees, and more enlightened thinking, have made it harder for employers to sack employees for disrespect. The demand for respect from juniors greatly influences the way in which those in power might act. Juniors need to know the correct code for communicating their respect.

There is, as well, an interdependence in most societies. It takes many forms, from the welfare state to common interest clubs or societies. Most people have a need to live and work with others, and this requires us to modify what we do and say.

HOW PERSONAL VALUES AFFECT COMMUNICATION

Let's consider reasoning, for a start. In the West, we rely on logical argument. Facts and reason are paramount, and they can speak for themselves. However, the boss or leader can always say, 'This is what we are going to do' and everyone falls in line. It's the western way, and most people in the West have been conditioned from their earliest years to accept it. The East is different. There the preference is for influencing, through harmony. 'Do as I say' is too harsh for the East. Even seniors will 'hint' rather than order. Juniors will tend to avoid saying anything directly negative. Some will even take the blame for something not happening, or going wrong, rather than letting the boss know that he was at fault.

Phillip's mother was very eastern in her ways, while he is much more western. Their relationship was often affected by the East-West clash. For example, if she wanted a lift into town, she would never ask outright. Instead, she would say something like, 'I must take these curtains back to the store. Can I get a bus there from the top of the road?' All the while, she had no intention of taking the bus, but did not like to ask for a lift and risk rejection, which would cause her to lose face. On the other hand, Phillip knew full well what she was doing, and felt that she was manipulating him. 'If you want a lift,' he would say, 'just ask.'

It is less clear-cut when considering abstract values.

Both the Indian and the Chinese minds seem to take a position different from the western one when it comes to the need for defining truth. Westerners raised with an 'absolute' concept of truth would find it hard to understand that some nations have a less rigid approach. For example, one Scandinavian manager working in the East learned that 'I didn't do it' did not mean the physical action had not taken place. It merely meant that the individual had not meant or intended to do so. He was not denying responsibility for the action, only for the outcome. We may suppose he was lying, but he did not believe he was, because there was no wilful intent to cause the consequence of his action. It seems that, for the Chinese mind, questions related to truth are not relevant. Neither Indians nor Chinese regard truth as an absolute concept, in the way that westerners do. Does that surprise you? Then consider this.

We introduced a Jewish friend of ours, Michael, to David, a Methodist minister. Michael asked David, 'You're a priest. Tell me, are you allowed to lie?' Without a pause, David replied, 'Oh yes. There is such a thing as situational ethics. Essentially it means that you can do or say what is appropriate for the situation. You may ask me a question and I may decide that you are not entitled to know the answer. So I may give you whatever answer I deem appropriate at the time. It's simply another way of telling you to mind your own business.'

When we were in Malawi, a western ambassador told us that if we were asking someone in the street for directions, never to phrase the question as, 'Is this the way to Lilongwe?'. The answer would always be yes, whether it happened to be true or not. 'They want to please,' said the ambassador. 'So always ask, Where does this road lead? Then you'll get a more useful answer.'

CONFUCIUS HAD A PRAGMATIC APPROACH

So the Indian, Chinese, African ways, and situational ethics in the West, all have something in common: they will tell you what they think you should know, without any intention to deceive maliciously. Their good intentions transcend the facts. For them, truth is not absolute. This pragmatic approach to life is characterised by the teachings of **Confucius**, who must be counted among the most influential people of all time. Two of his most significant concepts were *Jen* and *Li*. *Jen* is the superior drive that separates man from animals. It gave rise to filial piety and respect for elders, and developed into a national cult by certain Confucian followers. Confucius stressed the importance of living by noble values, and said, 'The superior man is concerned with virtue; the inferior man is concerned with land. The superior man understands what is right; the inferior man understands what is profitable.'

Li equates to a wide range of terms in the English language, from decorum and formality to rituals. Confucius believed that correct form would restore elegance and order to society. This led to the elaborate politeness in Chinese social dealings.

In short, Confucius taught attitudes and behaviour that set standards both for the individual and for society, and required seniors (such as the ruler or the boss or the head of the family) to set a good example. His message for rulers was, 'To govern is to set things right. If you begin by setting yourself right, who will dare to deviate from the right?'

Among the other useful lessons from Confucius are these:

1. The **stability of society** is based on unequal relationships between people; relationships are based on mutual and complementary obligations. The junior

partner owes the senior respect and obedience. The senior owes the junior partner protection and consideration.

2. **The family** is the prototype of all social organisations. A person is first and foremost a member of a family and not an individual. Children should learn to restrain themselves, to overcome their individuality so as to maintain the harmony in the family.

3. **Virtuous behaviour** towards others consists of 'not treating others as one would not like to be treated oneself'. It is the same thought as 'Do unto others as you would have them do unto you', just expressed in the opposite way. Similarly, Confucian teaching does not instruct us to love our enemies as it does in the Christian religion. Rather, it enjoins us to 'Love men'.

4. Virtue with regard to our **tasks in life** consists of trying to acquire skills and education, working hard, not spending more than necessary, being patient, and persevering. Conspicuous consumption is taboo, as is losing one's temper. There should be moderation in enjoying all things.

Chinese values may seem strange to westerners, at first, but glance down this checklist of values, and you will probably identify with most, if not all, of them:

- thrift
- persistence and perseverance
- having a sense of shame
- having few desires
- moderation and following the middle way

- adaptability
- prudence (carefulness)
- tolerance of others
- harmony with others
- non-competitiveness
- trustworthiness
- contentment with one's position in life
- solidarity with others
- being conservative
- chastity in women
- patriotism
- patience
- courtesy
- kindness (forgiveness, compassion).

ISSUES RELATING TO RELIGION

There is a philosophical divide between the eastern and western religions. The eastern religions are Hinduism, Buddhism, Shintoism, Taoism. The western religions are Judaism, Christianity, and Islam. The three western religions belong to the same family and therefore share a common factor. All three are based on the existence of the truth, which is accessible only to the true believer. In the east, there is no major religion which is based on the belief in a truth that a human community can embrace. They offer various ways in which a person can improve him/herself – however these do not consist in believing, but rather of ritual meditation as ways of living. Some of these may lead to a higher spiritual state and eventually to unification with God or gods. Therefore, asking somebody what he believes is an irrelevant question in the East. What one *does* is what matters.

CORE BELIEFS, ACCEPTING NEW, DROPPING OLD

Muslim countries are still searching for ways of coping with modern life. The Muslim countries of the Middle East, in spite of all their enormous oil riches, have hardly adapted better to the modern world than those which remained poor. Christian countries entered the road to modernisation with the Renaissance and the Reformation – while the Muslim world retreated into traditionalism. Contrary to what happens in East Asia and the West, many opinion leaders in the Middle East seem to interpret modern technology and western ideas as a threat rather than as an opportunity.

They mistakenly assume that progress can only be at the expense of their traditions. The Finns, in contrast, despite clinging to some old traditions, are very modern – always adopting new technology and ideas.

THE REASONING PROCESS

Apart from language and attitudes, there are certain practices and thought processes that characterise nations. Different cultures reason, process information, and work things out in quite different ways. This is important to understand when problem solving with people from another culture. One set of people will see only the tangible evidence, while another will work with hypotheses. The former relate everything to their own experience, and look for similarities, and for this reason we can call their thinking *grounded*. The other group is capable of abstract ideas and reasoning that may extend beyond the obvious, so we may call their reasoning *free-flowing*. Clearly, a free-flowing thinker could easily become impatient with a group of grounded thinkers, while they might consider him a dangerous speculator.

There is no universal rule, but broadly the reasoning styles are:

1. **Open-minded**: seeks more information before making a decision.

2. **Closed-minded**: selects and interprets data electively and ignores the rest.

3. **Associative**: relates new information to personal experience.

4. **Abstractive**: can handle new data and extrapolate from it.

5. **Individualistic**: make decisions that relate to themselves.

6. **Collectivist**: make decisions by consensus.

7. **Deductive**: works from the general to the particular.

8. **Inductive:** works from the particular to the general.

Let's consider a few of these in slightly greater detail.

People are either **open-minded** or **closed-minded**, and sometimes we are pleasantly surprised when we expect them to be closed but they turn out to be open-minded. North Americans may sound open-minded, but they are actually the opposite. Their world is contained within their national borders, and the vast majority of the ordinary citizens of America and Canada neither know nor care about what happens across the oceans. Fundamentalist societies such as the Muslim states and the few remaining monarchies may also tend towards closed-mindedness, because they believe that their way is the only right one. Such people will not be very receptive to points of view that differ from their own. However, the citizens of former repressive regimes (such as Russia, East Germany and Yugoslavia) will tend to be open-minded as they race to catch up with the rest of the free world.

♦ An **open-minded person** seeks to persuade, whereas a **closed-minded person** will continue the discussion to obtain more information and test out the validity of what has already been learned. The other person will say, 'Stop wasting time. My mind is made up. Don't confuse me with facts!'

♦ **Individualistic** people will seek to serve their self interest, while the **collectivists** will search for a solution that is for the common good. They will never agree on what is best...unless they can first agree on a common purpose.

♦ **Inductive:** Starting with attention to facts, data, and details which, when accepted, allow the discussion to move on to more general principles. In simple terms, it means moving from particular examples to a general principle, and requires the kind of thinking that can spot a pattern and expect it to apply to situations that have not yet been observed. It's a reasoning style that is widely used by the Americans, English and Northern Europeans.

- ◆ **Deductive**: This is the opposite kind of reasoning, moving from the general to the specific. The emphasis is on statements of principle, and checking that the situation being considered matches the general or governing principle. In discussions, deductive reasoners place great importance on citing recognised authorities and precedents. Implicitly they are saying, 'We know this to be true because it happened before. We will accept the new situation only if it matches what went before.' Russians, French, and Latins think this way.

Some nations regard personal and family relationships as most important, and will disregard the law or other rules in favour of those relationships (<u>particular</u> thinkers). Others believe that laws and rules are paramount for the good of society (<u>universalist</u> thinkers). Different nations do not all process information the same way, but most fall into two broad camps:

1. **Particularist.** These people look at each situation on its own merits. They include Egyptians, French, Greeks, Chinese, Portuguese, Mexicans, Singaporeans.

2. **Universalist.** These people look for universal rules or laws to govern their decisions and behaviour. They include Australians, Brazilians, Canadians, Finns, Germans, Britons, Swedes, Americans.

Another important point of difference is in the use of commonplace terms. Everyone knows the obvious examples, such as the US–UK conflict over the use of 'table a topic': Americans mean 'drop it from the agenda' while Brits mean 'add it'. However, there are many more possibilities for confusion in less obvious situations, and sometimes what the speaker says may not be what the listener hears. They may both process information differently. Consider this dialogue:

> Negative question: 'Isn't my dinner ready yet?'
> Westerner: 'No.' (= No, it's not yet ready)
> Chinese: 'Yes.' (= Yes, it's not yet ready)

The trap for the westerner in the East is that a Malaysian's response would also be 'No', just like his own – confusing, because he might think a Malaysian looks Chinese.

Interestingly, a nation's language reflects its thinking style.

◆ **English** writing and thinking is linear and follows logic.

◆ **Semitic** languages (Arabic and Hebrew) use parallels of thought.

◆ **Orientals** communicate indirectly and think in a decreasing spiral.

◆ **Romance** languages sway between opposites.

Doing – The English language is very action orientated; Americans and Anglo-Saxons are ready to get going from the start. We use a lot of action verbs and the active voice – 'I did it' rather than 'It was done'.

Thinking – Euro rationals use rhetoric and allow you time

to think through the argument and consequences; they use conceptual thinking. Likewise, Oriental languages use metaphors to get people to think, perhaps partly because directness is considered impolite, and partly because it is more valuable to understand the message without having it spelt out.

Being – Some cultures, especially in the Middle East, are very fatalistic. Their speech reflects the attitude that they have no control to influence any outcome. Eastern Europeans also think similarly after years of communism.

Broadly, the difference between East and West in communication styles is that:

- ◆ The West uses logic and argument to get others to agree (= factual and appeals to the head).

- ◆ Asian culture tries to influence through harmony and peer pressure (= relationship, thus appealing to the emotions).

5

Some Influences on Behaviour

'Long delays no longer mattered. The threat of passing time was an idea alien to them. So what if time passed, it was a gift, like life and energy and speech, to be spent lavishly on those around them.'

(Mary Cole, *Dirtroads: Footloose in Africa*)

Let's take a look at some of the characteristics of different nations, to help our understanding of how they approach certain sensitive social issues.

RULES
Broadly, there are two approaches to rules – **standardised** and **elitist**.

◆ **Standardised**. In the countries that favour a standardised approach, laws are well formed and codified, and equality before the law is accepted and universally applied. However, each nation applies its own degree of flexibility in observing the law. American culture, for example, is famous for standardisation. Americans like to create policies and procedures that can be applied everywhere. When they acquire foreign companies, they say: Do it the American way – regardless of local situation. This same attitude is applied to rule-keeping. For them it means observing the American attitude to procedures and to authority, which involve a degree of independent thought, i.e. observing the spirit, more than the letter, of the law.

This individualistic interpretation of the law has created a huge market for lawyers. America has lots of lawyers, whose lucrative role is to ensure that all the individual self interests don't break contracts. Law is a superimposed system that has not necessarily been sanctioned by pre-existing culture or society, and the Americans' litigious tendency is a way of asserting the rights of the individual over the system.

The Finns, on the other hand are the best at keeping to the rules. They cross the road at traffic lights only when the little green man lights up, and they frown at those who dare to cross at other times. Their belief in correct behaviour runs deep, affecting even their personal standards of integrity. It makes Finns the most honest people in the world. If you leave your handbag or wallet in a public place, it will still be there when you return hours later.

◆ **Elitist**. Being part of the elite in some cultures means being above the law. Elites have the power to influence – and they see nothing wrong in wielding that influence in ways that some nations might regard as corrupt. Many hierarchical societies have a tendency towards elitism, which is a close parallel to ambition and success motivation. Wherever there is a ladder of success there will be elitism, but some nations are more prone to that tendency than others. They are the ones who believe that the more successful or socially important you are, the less you are bound by the rules.

DIFFERENT DISCIPLINES

The French create countless rules and regulations – and spend their time trying to find ways around them. Others call them arrogant because they follow the rules only when it suits them, while insisting that everyone else should remain bound by them. Greeks are infamous in the EU for never obeying the directives! The French and the Greeks are clearly elitist in one sense, the Germans in another. They love orderliness, clear instruction, and efficiency, but are noted for solving problems by promulgating regulations. In effect, they are saying: We know best. As mentioned above, Americans believe that regulatory laws are instruments to be used and manipulated to solve problems. Hispanics view law as an expression of the ideal, almost a work of art, which may be admired and appreciated but which does not necessarily apply to them personally.

In Northern Europe it is culture, quite apart from the law, that provides a sin-and-guilt control mechanism based on the Protestant ethic and on Calvinist preaching. Religion exists to define right and wrong, and set rules for moral and ethical behaviour. The law must therefore be consistent with religious doctrine, in those northern countries.

In Southern Europe, shame tends to be the control mechanism. A person's relationships with other people and with the group will determine acceptable behaviour. Bad behaviour will lead to judgement, condemnation, and ultimately exclusion from the group. Ethics is more related to the situation and who is involved. As films like *The Godfather* showed, respect played a large part amongst Sicilians, and the lack of respect could lead to punishment.

In Asia, face, honour, dignity and obligation are all strong agents for controlling behaviour, quite apart from the law. Eastern cultures are based on centuries-old customs based on those values, and should there ever be a conflict between the law (recent) and customs (ancient), the latter will determine how the Asian behaves.

Religions are important too. In Hindu and Buddhist societies, religious systems play an important role in regulating behaviour, even with people who do not actively practise any religion. In one approach to the law, it doesn't matter what the evidence is, nor what you said to the police in your statement. What counts is what you say in front of the judge – as this is seen as being between you and your God.

LEADERSHIP

There are a number of well known patterns of leadership, each reflecting the culture of its adherents. Two group-ings, in particular, exemplify the East–West divide:

◆ **Hierarchical**. This style requires everyone to know and remain in his or her place. Decision-making is autocratic and obedience is valued and expected. It applies mainly in the Middle East, Latin America and Asia, and works for the mass of the people, but not for those with the ambition to succeed on their own merits. Conversely, the majority of people who accept such a leadership style also expect their superiors to lead – and to take the decisions. They are very disconcerted by a consultative approach to management.

- **Flat** leadership acknowledges equality among people, but the locus of leadership may shift according to expertise. We all contribute as equals, but in certain circumstances, those who know best are expected to show the way. American organisations have levels or steps of power but the management structures are fairly flat. The UK is slightly more hierarchical, but Nordic and Dutch organisations have very flat patterns of authority. First among equals, if you know what I mean.

STATUS

- **Achieved**. This orientation is characteristic of western cultures, reflecting the drive to better ourselves and gain the recognition we have earned.

- **Ascribed**. In other, older types of societies, who you are is important, not whether you are any good at the job. It applies widely in the Middle East, Asia, Latin America. Even France has a penchant for this orientation – people from *les Grandes Ecoles* are probably even more snobbish than Old Etonians or Oxbridge graduates ever were.

It is said that this attitude exists also in Argentina, combined with the 'know your place' set of values. The effect is to inhibit initiative and block the emergence of new talent, because those in authority seek to accumulate rather than delegate power, and value social status more than achievement.

RISK/UNCERTAINTY

◆ **Inelastic**. Some nations don't like change and uncertainty. They dislike taking risks. For them, traditions and customs reduce the uncertainty in life. Greece, Portugal, Belgium and many Latin American countries are this way. France cherishes its bureaucracies. Unless you can show them a negligible downside, negotiations can drag on forever.

◆ **Elastic**. Britain, the celebrated nation of shopkeepers, is full of risk takers who can live with uncertainty. They can be flexible and manage by trial and error. Americans thrive even more on trial and error. For them there's always a new and better way of doing things. Flexibility and adaptability have become high priorities in Italy and Spain to bring about better economic performance. Such nations respond well to new and exciting ideas. It is no accident that Finland is so advanced in its use of new technology: their nation's motto seems to be 'there's always a better way'.

PRIVACY

◆ **Open**. We Brits readily share information about ourselves to others. We are like an open book, and appear informal and extrovert, although there is a closed door not far below the surface. Americans seem even more open. However, this is because their mobility creates a need to form fast but short-lived relationships, with many acquaintances but few deep friendships.

- **Closed**. Many European peoples are introverted, formal and difficult to know. They can seem very evasive. Yet, over time they develop strong, intimate relationships and their friends are embraced within a wider family. They are suspicious of any get-in-quick approach, and resent forced familiarity, uninvited use of first names and intrusion into their personal space bubble.

INDIVIDUAL VERSUS THE GROUP

- **Individual**. Certain societies (mainly New World) value the uniqueness of each person. They encourage their children to be different, take personal responsibility, be self-reliant, and express their individual opinions and talent. Achieving their own potential is paramount. Their group is loosely structured, relying on individual guilt/conscience for social control. Rewards are based on personal achievement, and they believe that when individuals pursue their own goals, ultimately the group will benefit.

  Americans are regarded as number one in the world at individuality. Above all, they cherish freedom of choice, opportunity and self-expression. When they speak and think about self-development they mean themselves – not you.

- **Group**. In group-based societies, however, personal identity is expressed through the social group, e.g. family, class, clan, caste. The Japanese take the view that individuality is immature, and required by people who haven't grown up enough. In Japan rewards are based on loyalty and how close we can become to the 'head' of the relevant group. Affiliations are important, and such considerations as personal security, financial well-being and prestige are closely linked to membership of the group. The Mafia have a similar approach. Group-based societies discourage the pursuit of private self-interests, because they are not good for the group. Loyalty and duty are prized, and decisions are taken only after collective discussion, even if they are taken by the most senior person.

ACHIEVEMENT

America (and nations that follow the US example) rate personal achievement very highly. Rags-to-riches stories have great currency there, with the emphasis on happy endings and rewards for achievement. It's a positive, optimistic outlook, often described as a 'can do' attitude. It's egalitarian, with an emphasis on self-help and applied knowledge.

There is no society that actively discourages achievement, although socialist/communist doctrines did seek to suppress individuality, and some nations are still suspicious of anyone who tries to stand out from the crowd. The only difference is that such societies prefer collective success to individual achievement. People in former communist countries sometimes find it difficult to respond as individuals, preferring to shelter behind their job responsibilities.

At a recent conference held in Russia, Debbie learned at first hand the implications of this. She was aghast to find that she was the only speaker who talked about opportunities and solutions, whereas the other speakers focused only on problems and obstacles. She wondered whether this was because their nation is still in the middle of their problems or whether it demonstrated a fundamental emphasis on thinking about process and not achievement.

There are major differences between Britain and her European neighbours, and not only over the common currency. The defining characteristic of the British people is *achievement*.

British society programmes its citizens to value and seek achievement, rewarding those who succeed, while scorning those who fear to attempt. Shakespeare expressed the British approach well in these words:

> 'Our doubts are traitors
> And make us lose the good we oft might win
> By fearing to attempt.'
> (*Measure for Measure*)

The clear implication of those words is that it is wrong to hesitate and right to take the plunge. Such an approach makes for a competitive environment in which there are choices, and in which value is placed on hard work and knowledge. Achievement is measured by the symbols of success: cars, houses, jewellery, membership of golf clubs, and foreign holidays. Quality of life is expressed in terms of material comforts rather than spiritual progress or the intangibles that bring greater contentment than the rewards of the rat race.

In contrast, those from Catholic countries such as Italy, Spain and Portugal, place much greater emphasis on the way people relate to each other. Their emphasis is on managing connections with other people rather than on managing things. Being who you are counts more than what you achieve. The tendency towards reciprocal relationships is reflected in the existence of the Mafia and its code of obligation for favours given.

HISTORICAL

One important consideration, in understanding East–West attitudes is the colonial legacy. Former colonies in Africa, Asia and the Caribbean have a certain ambivalence: they resent their former colonial masters while cherishing their western ways. For example, they might be proud of their command of English (and possibly their English accent too) while being quick to resent any implication that they should be subservient to the 'mother country'.

This attitude is strongly evident when they play (and beat) England at Cricket or some other sport. It spills over into business dealings too.

VALUE-SETS

Peter Cochrane (previously head of BT's innovation centre) said the difference between East and West is noticed when you relate your values. His values are:

- first, wife
- then family,
- eventually ending with contribution to the betterment of the UK.

However, Japanese businessmen want:

- to contribute to Japanese society to serve the greater glory of Japan
- then enhance the profit of the company.
- the last thing on the list is his wife.

GENDER ISSUES
In Muslim countries there is a strict allocation of space to each sex. Public places are for men only – if women enter (e.g. go out in the street) they are trespassing on male territory. Women are restricted to a few locations and must wear a veil. In effect, it means that the woman is present in the man's world, but invisible, because she has no right to be in the street.

Women in male spaces are considered provocative and offensive, upsetting the male's order and committing an act of aggression against men. By entering the male space they are being assertive, and assertiveness in women is not considered acceptable in what is essentially a chauvinistic society. (This attitude is not uniquely Muslim. Consider the likely reactions, in Britain, if women were to turn up at a Round Table Meeting or a Freemason's Lodge – with a few exceptions, these have long been regarded as male preserves.)

There is no accepted pattern for interactions between unrelated men and women. In orthodox societies, men mustn't touch and mustn't look. Two British businessmen had an audience with an Arab prince with whom they were seeking to conclude a deal. Also in the room was the Prince's stunningly beautiful wife. One of the business-men could not take his eyes off her. The next day he was instructed to leave the country immediately. The Prince had taken offence at the man staring at his wife.

One of our trainers was conducting a programme in Dubai on PR and media relations. Three of the delegates were Muslim women, complete with head scarves. During one of the breaks, as they were sitting around having a coffee, the trainer lightly touched one of the women on the upper arm during a conversation. There was a sharp intake of breath around the table, and he quickly apologised. Remember that books on body language (in the West) will indicate that it is socially safe to touch a member of the opposite sex on any part of the arm (except the hand).

The upshot of all this is the need to be sensitive to cultural differences, and to err on the side of caution, avoiding familiarity of any kind, and taking your lead from the other person. Even though the younger generation in orthodox societies (Middle East, Japan, China, etc.) may be tending to accept social equality, they retain their respect for their elders, and will therefore react as their seniors would wish.

Their American accent and a Harvard MBA may lull you into expecting western ways. However, the pull of tradition will usually override modern behaviour, not least because it enables them to score points by rapping you over the knuckles if you overstep the mark.

EQUALITY ISSUES

Inequality exists everywhere. Many emerging nations have a rich elite who have the education, the farms and factories. Some nations discriminate against women. Others look down on minorities on the grounds of their skin colour, race or religion. In his Gettysburg Address, Abraham Lincoln may have said that all men are equal, but in practice it ain't necessarily so. Such attitudes of discrimination will colour the way people negotiate or respond to business approaches from foreigners who resemble the minority they habitually discriminate against at home.

LEGAL SYSTEMS

Even legal systems are different. In some countries you are presumed innocent until proven guilty, while in others the reverse applies. Unlike England, Scotland has a 'not proven' verdict. Plane spotters in Greece can find themselves charged with espionage and thrown in jail. Holidaymakers who become drunk and disorderly in other countries could find themselves in far greater trouble than they ever imagined. The European Union may have sought to create a uniform Europe, but it has not yet eliminated these variations in practices. Brussels may decree all it likes, but local culture will prevail for many years to come.

BEING SENSITIVE TO DIFFERENT NORMS

Norms are different in every country. In one country it

may be a small matter to travel on a train without a ticket. In another, it could result in a large fine just for not having passed your ticket through a machine at the start of your journey. Women risk official wrath in some countries just by dressing lightly in hot weather, and Arab women would avoid being photographed without a *burka*, if the photo was likely to end up in one of the more fundamentalist countries. Western tourists unthinkingly wander into mosques with their shoes on. Grey hairs earn more respect in some cultures than others.

All of this underlines the variations in lifestyle, in expectations, and in going about business in countries that are geographically close but culturally distant. What does it mean for you? It means that you need to be wary when seeking to do business or spend time abroad. It would take weeks to educate you in all the ways of a single foreign country, let alone the many that you might visit or deal with. So we shall not attempt such a major undertaking.

Rather, we shall cover those important differences that can make or break a business relationship, and try to create in you a sensitivity to cultural differences. If we had to offer you a single word to guide your attitude to those differences, that word would be **respect**. If you place respect in your personal filter, and pass all considerations through it, you won't go far wrong.

6

The Five Stages of Cultural Learning

'Is this communication within the recipient's range of perception? Can he receive it?'
(Peter Drucker)

When we enter a new environment, most of us take a little while to learn how to fit in with the host community. Often through making mistakes we learn what works and what does not, if we wish to gain acceptance. Typically, there are five stages to get through:

1. catch up
2. relating
3. shock
4. understanding
5. progress.

Before addressing them let's remind ourselves of some aspects of culture shock that are so obvious that we may not recognise their cultural connections:

♦ When you notice some violation of social rules or norms, you tend to attribute it to the ignorance of those responsible (for example, queue jumping or not buying a ticket before boarding a train).

- If those violations persist, you suspect that those responsible are being deliberately anti-social or even dishonest (e.g. you may have a prejudice against certain races and view such transgressions as simply confirmation of your opinion that they are fundamentally dishonest/selfish/anti-social – 'Typical..!').

- Only later, and perhaps after receiving some insight, might you consider that they may have a different set of rules or values.

- The more similar two cultures are, the greater the shock when discrepancies appear, such as between the British and either the Americans or the Australians. Because they speak the same language and have the same historical background, you expect them to behave like you, with the same level of diffidence, politeness, or sense of formality. They don't.

- Cultural friction is aggravated by communication breakdowns, which can result from something as simple as not understanding the accent or speech pattern of the other person. Some languages do not seem to have a word for 'please', so they always sound bossy or impolite when speaking English.

- Groups look for third parties to act as referees or arbitrators when they cannot communicate with each other.

- People who communicate effectively usually get their own way. Others leave it to them to speak for the group, to ask or negotiate for what they need. This is true among English speakers, but even more likely when trying to cope in a foreign country, speaking a foreign language.

♦ People become embarrassed when having to communicate in some 'new' way (remember learning a foreign language at school? Remember how difficult it was to stand up in class and answer the teacher's question in the foreign language?).

♦ Time spent on improving your communication skills is frequently more valuable than time spent on tasks or 'doing'. Just to be able to make yourself understood – and to understand – liberates you and helps you to feel you can cope and make things happen.

Now let's take a look at the vicious and virtuous spirals of fitting in with a new host community. Remember that these apply equally to Brits going to another country, and foreigners coming to Britain. What is important is to understand the process that occurs.

VIRTUOUS SPIRAL
This provides the insight to fit in, and it works something like this:

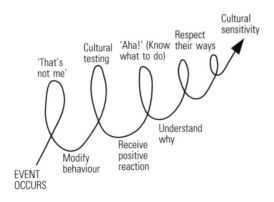

Virtuous Spiral

Chiang arrived in London from Singapore and contacted an English family he had met back home. They invited him to join them for tea at a well-known hotel in central London, and he made a point of arriving exactly at 3.30 in the afternoon. His hosts introduced him to a couple of their friends, then ordered tea with cucumber sandwiches and cakes, and the conversation revolved around family and friends, until the food and tea arrived. Chiang was astute enough to wait and watch, before helping himself, and he noticed that the English took a small cake or sandwich and placed it on the small plate in front of them, leaving it there for a short while before starting to eat it. Chiang's Chinese way would have been to take a cake or sandwich from the central plate and eat it immediately. He said to himself, 'This is different. It's not how the Chinese eat.' (*Not like us.*)

Although he was amused by the practice of looking at the food before eating it, Chiang realised that it was probably the custom in England. He copied their example. (*Modified behaviour.*) The next time he had a meal with some English people, he watched for a repetition of the take-place-look-eat sequence, and found it generally repeated, but more among the older people, and not always by the young. Once or twice he noticed a youth being corrected by his parent for eating straight off the central plate. (*Cultural testing.*) He believed he had learned a new behaviour and understood that it was the correct form in polite society in England, (*Aha!*) although he still did not know why. Some time later, when he was with someone he could trust not to mock his question, he asked about the practice, and was told, 'It's the polite way. If everyone just eats straight off the central plate, it would be like feeding time at the trough on the pig farm.' (*Understanding why.*)

Knowing the reason for the custom, and understanding its social effect helped Chiang to fit more easily into his new social setting. He respected the English way and developed a sensitivity to their social customs, realising that they were about not appearing self-centred or greedy. That was the *insight* which helped him to integrate better into the host community. At first he laughed at the practice, but in time it became his own learned behaviour, and he found himself correcting others who did not follow suit. Importantly, his starting point was his *willingness* to learn and adopt the local ways.

Phillip had a similar experience in his first job in England. Sailing from Calcutta in company with some English people who had just retired from senior jobs in Calcutta, he regularly joined them for a beer before lunch. He understood that to be the norm, the Calcutta way: beer *before* lunch.

Soon after starting work in North London, he was invited to join his supervisor, Bob, for lunch, 'And afterwards we can pop into the pub for a pint.' His response was to say, 'But surely one doesn't drink beer *after* lunch?' To which Bob replied, 'This one does!' Phillip soon realised that his other colleagues would pop into the pub after eating, if they had time. Food was more important, so they would take care of that first, then have a drink if time permitted. It made sense. And it made even more sense to follow their example, instead of pointing out that other societies did things differently.

Working with Scandinavian groups, helping them to develop their communication skills, it became obvious to us that they believed in the efficiency of their own ways and could not understand why their (obvious) rules could not be understood/accepted/acted upon by the Orientals and Africans they dealt with. Almost without exception, when asked about their approach to communication, they would focus on what *they* had to say, and the way they chose to say it. If they wanted help, it was always to clarify their message, sharpen their delivery, make their case more succinctly. It was never about understanding the communication style of people they were addressing, and what their expectations might be. In short, it was one-way traffic, and that's not a dialogue!

VICIOUS SPIRAL

The vicious spiral produces bruising, and it can create a block to fitting in, by causing a person to revert to his/her own way of doing things. It might work like this:

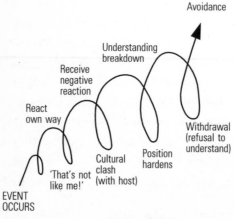

Vicious Spiral

One Scandinavian member of the diplomatic service who was temporarily posted to Malawi was almost immediately at odds with the Africans. Punctuality was one of his fixations. The Malawians had quite a different sense of timekeeping. The Scandinavian became impatient with them and commented crossly whenever the Africans were late. He expected them to fit in with his sense of timing, and considered them lazy and inefficient for not being punctual.

His main error was in judging their behaviour by his own Scandinavian standards – and in letting them see and hear his displeasure. He wasn't interested in understanding their ways and their thinking. Needless to say this made him no friends, and his temporary stay in Malawi was not a success. Even before he had left the country he was openly dismissive of their unpunctual ways and what he considered their lack of drive and purpose. What's more, he did not want to make the effort to understand or accept their ways. He preferred to get away. He had descended all the way down the vicious spiral.

Now let's take a look at the five stages of cultural learning which are implicit in the virtuous and vicious spirals.

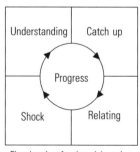

Five levels of cultural learning

- **Catch up** involves a recognition that we do not do things in the same way as the host community, and need to learn new ways. It is the process of watching, copying and fitting in. The first requisite must be a willingness to change or adapt our own ways. Often, older and less worldly members of certain communities prefer not to make the effort, staying among their own kind and speaking only their own language. This is not a recommended route for anyone wishing to do business within the host community! The process of catching up may involve some discomfort while it lasts, but it is always necessary and need not last long.

- **Relating** means connecting with others. This is very useful, because it allows us to accelerate the process of cultural adaptation. Friends (even new ones) will tell us more than we can learn for ourselves, and if we keep ourselves open to new thinking we will accept the guidance and feedback we receive. Inevitably, we will start with some erroneous impressions, even if we have done our homework and read all the right books. The pace of change is tremendous, and even some of the well-known national characteristics mentioned in this book will soon be out of date. It would therefore be useful to get the current picture from new friends and colleagues in the host community.

- **Shock.** Inevitably, things will sometimes go wrong. A social gaffe or a cultural mistake in a business meeting may set you back. Or it may be that some local practice will catch you unawares, and you may take offence. For example, some countries have a very childish sense of humour, and think nothing of poking fun at one another in a way that a Brit might consider personally insulting. When such an incident occurs, the temptation is to take offence. However, it is always worth remembering that offence is in the intention. If you give offence without intending to, just apologise and explain. If someone else offends you, ask yourself if it was intended. If not, don't take offence.

◆ **Understanding**. Possibly the hardest part of the integration process is to set aside the reflex of rejecting anything that is 'not like us'. Once we can do this, it becomes easier to integrate. We must always operate within a country's range of values or risk being rejected. We must fit in and communicate in the vocabulary (of ideas as well as words) of the host community. For example, it's pointless applying your own standards in a country that has a different set of values. In Malawi we were intrigued to hear that they considered it normal to borrow parts from one another's cars to pass the annual car test, and then to return them so the next person could also pass the test. It was necessary for us to understand that they did not consider it wrong to do so.

◆ **Progress.** Finally, we come to personal growth. To understand and cope with cultural diversity is to make progress in our personal development. When we learn more about others we learn more about ourselves. Also, integration is a mature concept. It does not mean the same as assimilation, and it does not mean that we should all be the same. Rather, it means recognising and accepting cultural differences, and creating channels for two-way communication.

These five stages are also the measures of our cultural learning. They provide us with the insight and the mindset to fit in with the host community, and to overcome the barriers to clear communication across cultures.

7

When is a 'Yes' not a 'Yes'

'A firm may say, 'Yes, your shipment will be ready on Tuesday.' You arrive on Tuesday to pick it up but find it is not ready. No one is upset or embarrassed. Time commitments are considered desirable objectives but not binding promises.'

(Eva Kras, describing Mexico
Management in Two Cultures)

Much of business communication involves negotiation – for new business, for contracts, for employment, to satisfy customers, and so on. At root, it tends to be about persuading the other person to your point of view. So you are looking for a 'Yes' response.

The problem is, even if you get a 'Yes' from someone of a different cultural background, can you be sure it really means 'Yes'? Not only that, there will be times when the other person may say 'Yes' or nod repeatedly throughout your discussion or presentation, yet you could walk away without the agreement you thought you had. Nods and smiles all round...but no coconut!

Perhaps someone should tell Asians that when they say 'Yes' the whole world gets the wrong idea! Seriously, though, there are some cultural influences at work behind the responses of some Asians.

Ayesha was from the Indian sub-continent. Although she had lived in London for most of her life, she retained her Indian accent. It bothered her, and she wanted to lose it and sound like an educated English woman. She consulted *Yellow Pages* and called a couple of training companies specialising in communication skills, including ours.

'I am interested,' she said, 'in elocution lessons and public speaking.'

Our PA told her the daily fee, which is set at a corporate level, and usually seems high to a private individual. 'But she didn't flinch,' reported our PA. We called Ayesha back, as she had requested, to make arrangements, and left a message on her voice mail, but we never heard from Ayesha again.

Our PA was puzzled. 'She seemed so interested. I told her what we could do for her, told her the fee, and she didn't flinch. She wanted you to call her back and make an appointment to discuss her requirements, so I wonder why she never called us again.'

Phillip put on his Oriental face and told her, 'Ayesha is from the East. Probably comes from a well-off family. There are two reasons why she would not react to the fee you quoted. First, her background will have conditioned her not to show surprise or dismay, because that would be unsophisticated. Second, if she said she found the fee high, it would be like admitting she could not afford it. She could not do that without losing face.'

That's not so strange, if you think about it. Ever popped into a shop, or stopped by a market stall, to ask the price of something that caught your eye, and found the quoted price rather more than you expected? What did you say? Did you say, 'I'll think about it'? And did you actually mean, 'It's too much!'? Why didn't you say so? Probably because you did not want to appear unable to afford it. And because such an admission would have placed you in a lower spending bracket. I'm sure you would not like to be considered 'no big spender'. That would cause you to lose face.

In Asia, the need to avoid losing face is an important social and psychological reality, connected to the fact that the group takes precedent over the individual. To cause another to lose face would be to disrupt social harmony and be considered dishonourable, therefore, an indirect communication style is the norm. One western girl living with a Chinese family realised that after she kept getting blocking responses even in casual situations. She would sometimes ask whether she could go into town. If the family wanted to say 'no', the answer would be: the bus may be broken today. She wondered, How do they know? Why are they being so pessimistic? Do they not want me to travel by bus? Why? Until eventually she understood that they were denigrating the bus in order not to have to refuse her permission, because to do so would make her feel subject to their will and therefore inferior.

The essence of face is to avoid making the other person uncomfortable or to lose their personal dignity. It's a concept well known in the West, but probably not recognised for what it is. Consider this: you meet someone important and famous in a social context, and get on well, on equal terms. Later you discover how important that person is, but the relationship remains good. Then one day at work you make a mistake that upsets an important client – guess who? Now you have to encounter that celebrity, not as the new friend, but as the employee that made a mistake.

It's much worse than if you had never met socially, isn't it? Because now you will lose face. Of course, it could be that your celebrity friend will think no less of you than before, but the change will be in your own mind. *You* will feel that things have changed, and that they may never be the same again.

RECOGNISE EFFORTS TO SAVE YOUR FACE

Pay very careful attention to the other person's body language to see if you are coming up against an invisible cultural barrier. Asians find it very hard to say 'No', and will usually say 'Yes' with the full intention of trying to meet the obligation, even if they know it's unlikely to happen. Sometimes the lack of an answer is tantamount to a 'no'. In other instances, a 'yes' without a follow-up is a 'no'. Always pay more attention to the body language than the words, because their discomfort in such a situation will probably be evident.

If they say 'No' it may cause you to lose your standing – with them, with the group, with your employers – and thus to lose face. They would feel uncomfortable about being so rude or disrespectful, regardless of any difference in your respective social status, unless there was a clear master/servant relationship (in their favour). Also, it would tend to alter their relationship with you. When they say 'No' to you, they exercise power over you, placing you in the role of 'supplicant' which, in the East, is an inferior position. Some people find it hard to adopt a superior posture towards a friend or anyone other than a trades-man or servant, so they tend to wriggle and speak indirectly, to maintain the rhythm of harmony. A 'No' causes a block.

In contrast, the English language's directness can appear very hostile to some cultures. The 'say what you mean, and mean what you say' works well for us in our culture which is direct and individualistic – but causes great discomfort in collectivist and indirect cultures such as those found in Asia.

Bill Stanley came to understand that by default. After years of managing an international company, he travelled the world as a sales specialist sharing his knowledge and wisdom. One day, in Japan, he used a well-tried device often employed by western speakers and trainers. Describing a classic mistake, he asked the audience, 'Hands up. Who among you has ever been stupid enough to do such a thing?' Everyone froze. No one breathed or moved so much as a single eyebrow hair. Bill was baffled, but later someone explained that he had been asking them to admit publicly that they had been stupid – a certain way to lose face.

'I learned the lesson,' said Bill, 'so the next time I did it differently. I raised my own hand first and asked: Who among you has ever been stupid, *like me* – and done such a thing?' Every hand shot up. The audience did not wish Bill to lose face by being the only one to have made a mistake! Only then did Bill really learn the lesson.

Another sort of cross-cultural tangle occurred when Nokia sent an engineer to India, to develop local technical skills. He selected an Indian employee and proceeded to show him how the job should be done. Throughout the week, the Indian nodded to show he understood, and did not ask any questions. Of course, the Finn assumed all was well and, with typical Finnish efficiency, gathered together the rest of the Indian employees for a demonstration by his trainee of how it should be done.

It was a disaster. The Indian hadn't really learned the process, or even understood it, so he failed spectacularly and nearly died of embarrassment.

What had gone wrong? It had been a clear case of cultural clashing. During his initial demonstration the Finn had accepted his Indian trainee's nods to mean that he understood. That's what a Finnish trainee would have meant. What's more, if a Finnish trainee did not understand something, he would have asked questions. The Indian had asked no questions, so the Nokia man assumed he had understood. Essentially there are two issues concerning face here; first, and perhaps the most obvious, is that the Indian didn't want to own up to not understanding, and second, which is far deeper, the Indian didn't want the Finn to lose face. He couldn't be a good teacher if the Indian hadn't understood, and as the Finn was his superior that was not an acceptable conclusion.

The structure of Finnish society, including at work, is very flat – among the flattest in the world – and equality is taken for granted. Indian society, in contrast, is very hierarchical, with every inch of seniority highly prized for self-esteem and to mark progress and success. In the example above, the Finn was insensitive to hierarchy, status and seniority. He made an assumption that people were the same the world over.

Such false assumptions can badly affect international negotiations.

UNDERSTAND WHY ORIENTALS SAY 'YES'

A telling example of the difference between Western values and those in the East occurs in E M Forster's *A Passage to India*. Dr Aziz is summoned to the compound of the civil surgeon, Major Callendar. While he is there, two English ladies, Mrs Callendar and Mrs Lesley, emerge from the house and, assuming that Dr Aziz's carriage is their own, get into it and tell the driver to drive off, leaving Dr Aziz to travel on foot. He is too polite to remonstrate with the English women on their slight, because that would have put them in the wrong and caused them embarrassment. He was prepared to suppress his own self-respect on their account, because his upbringing would not allow him to state his position and cause discomfort to someone else.

Something similar happened to Phillip in London. Someone he knew from his university days in Calcutta (let's call him Ravi) invited him and his wife, June, to dinner at their flat in Belsize Village, North London. They sat and talked and time wore on, while Ravi's wife went in and out of the room in increasing distress. Finally, at 9 pm, she served some food, but she and Ravi ate nothing. It turned out that they were serving the small amount of food they had for themselves. Ravi had not told his wife about his invitation, and she was wondering why their friends were not leaving. In fact, Ravi must have hoped his guests would give up and leave. The problem was, if Phillip and June *had* risen to leave, Ravi might have felt insulted and asked, 'Isn't my food good enough for you?'

With the wisdom of passing years, Phillip has realised that Ravi, who was living in straitened circumstances at the time, had issued the invitation in order to sound grand and keep up the social standing they had shared in Calcutta.

It is the same kind of thinking that drives an Oriental to say 'Yes' to a proposition that he has no hope of meeting. Being unable to say 'No', he might go in over his head and agree to something that will cause him a great deal of grief. Of course, he will probably try to meet his obligation and turn himself inside out in doing so, but eventually he will have to let someone down.

Sometimes an Easterner will say 'Yes' too often and cause problems even if he manages to complete what he has undertaken to do, because his thinking is not as compartmentalised as it is in westerners. If he takes on a task (other than a social responsibility), he feels a sense of duty to complete it, and would lose face if he admitted that he could not do so, even if it took forever to complete!

An Indian copywriter was paired with an art director in a large advertising agency in London. Because he was a fast writer, account executives brought him one job after another. He never refused, and even worked long hours to complete the jobs in his in-tray. The problem was that the art director could not keep up with him and a log jam resulted. In frustration, one day he pleaded, 'You've got to say "No". You can't keep on taking every job that comes our way!'

In this case, the 'Yes' did mean 'Yes', but it should have meant 'No' – or at least 'Maybe'. But it arose from the same mindset that would have prevented the Indian copywriter from refusing a request for something unreasonable. He would have taken on the responsibility for the situation so as not to embarrass the other person. He did not have the brutality or self-centredness to say, in effect, 'It's your problem.'

So how should a westerner cope with people who do not know how to say 'No'? Probably the best idea is to give them space and allow them the possibility of 'changing their minds with dignity' if the need arises. One thing to bear in mind is that if an Asian or African undertakes to do something, but does not deliver and does not explain why, it could be because he is not able to fulfil his commitment, and does not know how to tell you. Or it could be that his 'Yes' meant 'I'll try'. You may have to check it out and find a diplomatic way of releasing him from the obligation and finding another solution.

8

Making English International

'An Australian man once visited the island and asked me when the stores were open, since it was afternoon and he hadn't seen a store open yet. Taken aback at what seemed a stupid question, I told him the obvious truth, "They're open when their doors are open." When I walked away I realized it was a question I would have asked myself when I first arrived on Fiji.'

(Craig Storti, *Figuring Foreigners Out*)

HOW TO BREAK DOWN BARRIERS TO INTERNATIONAL COMMUNICATION

Imagine being sent to Heaven as you read a brochure for your dream car. Imagine drooling over the pictures, your pulse racing as you picture yourself behind the wheel. Picture it outside your home, read how quickly it zooms from 0–60mph, yet how safe it is for your children, how masterful it makes you feel to drive, how luxurious it is with all those extras. 'Wow! I want some of that,' you say to yourself.

That's what the copywriter gets paid for: to make you want some of that. Now imagine that same brochure being written by the engineer who helped design the car. What would we read? Probably we'd find out about the torque ratios, the bore and stroke of the pistons, the efficiency of the engine's 24 valves.

Is that really going to quicken your breathing and inflame the desire within you to buy it? Probably not! But why not? After all, the engineer is talking about the same car, so why aren't you licking your lips?

Unless you are an engineer your perspectives are different. The copywriter and the engineer have different approaches to communicating the worthiness of the car. The difference in their communication is not about pronunciation or even language. The difference is in the mental software of the two writers. They have different filters.

In business we often have to address people from different nations or cultures. A little bit of homework tells us they use kilometres not miles, centigrade and not Fahrenheit, a socialist or capitalist government, and what is the nation's favourite food. We then feel confident enough to alter our speech and 'tailor' it to the target audience. We check out a few more facts and are ready to go. But are we really?

The sad fact is that the English speakers of this world are the worst at adapting their communication to meet the expectations of people from a foreign land. We are very poor at cross-cultural understanding. We think that, because everyone speaks English, they understand what we say. It isn't so.

IT'S NOT ENOUGH TO TRANSLATE THE WORDS ALONE

When we translate the words alone, our communication misses the mark. Different nations have very different attitudes, cultures and behavioural norms. For example, 'The American Way' is not universally acceptable, whatever the residents of the USA may think. And remember how Debbie discovered that *mañana* doesn't mean 'tomorrow', but 'not today'. Equally, the British stiff upper lip is more mocked than mimicked in many countries. So we need to be sensitive to other cultures and reframe our messages to suit our listeners.

It is no longer enough to speak English louder and slower. It is no longer enough to merely cut out the jargon and find the right words. If we are telling the story of the unpopular Edsel car in America, it is no longer enough to replace the Edsel in the story with a Lada or a Deux Chevaux for a European audience. Not only would the detail not be right, but the point of the story would not be relevant in certain countries. What the Americans accept as the moral of the story may not mean anything to the Russians or the French. And whatever *we* may consider the significance of the story may not be important to those others. Similarly, we have to accept that our own fundamental beliefs may not be universal truths. Just like the copywriter and the engineer, our approach to life and our understanding of what happens around us will be very different from that of a foreigner.

EVEN THE BASIC ASSUMPTIONS ARE DIFFERENT

Consider the law. We are so used to the concept of being innocent until proven guilty that most of us would find it impossible to live under a judicial system where the burden of proof is upon the defendant and not upon the State. Yet this is what happens in Italy, and much of Europe still lives by 'The Code Napoleon'.

Consider the concept of time. Psychiatrists and psychologists working with refugees are having to rethink their attitudes to counselling after finding time-line therapy of little use when their subjects think of time (past, present and future) as cyclical or circular, and not linear, as we do in the West.

Consider the concept of individuality. As descendants of the Anglo-Saxons/Celts, Brits are very proud of their individuality, encouraging their children to think and be different. The Americans are the most individualistic nation in the world, having adopted the Anglo-Saxon model despite their racial mix; but the Japanese look upon individuality as immaturity. And if you were to venture into rural areas of Asia, you would be struck by the sheer pleasantness of the people and the absence of sarcasm or point-scoring in their speech. That could be because they do not have the values of individualistic people.

These are the types of things that characterise the core of our belief systems. They colour our language, signal our interpretation of events, and eventually determine our behaviour. Much of what we say, do, and feel is so ingrained in us that we do not realise that cultural conditioning has had a deep effect on us. We give out taught responses, but we can be taught new ones.

CONDITIONED (AND LIMITED?) BY THOSE AROUND US

A few years ago in London, Debbie stood admiring a beautiful landscape painting by the artist Constable. A man standing beside her turned and said, 'I used to hate his pictures. You see, I'm colour blind and, as a child, my elderly aunt used to make me stand in front of pictures for hours until I could 'appreciate them'. Of course, I never could or did – not while she was alive.' His story had a happy ending when he met a sympathetic art teacher at senior school who taught him to value everything about the paintings apart from the colours.

Debbie says, 'When I was younger, I disliked classical music intensely because I couldn't whistle, hum or sing it. But over the years I have learned to appreciate it because I now listen at a different level and for different things. I didn't just come by this understanding; I was taught it.'

Cultural understanding, similarly, is something we can all develop. The first step is to understand that others think, believe and feel differently from ourselves, and it will enable us to understand ourselves better. Whether we are talking about business and management, work/life balance, medicine and healing, selling, negotiation, or education, the people we encounter abroad will have a set of values that will differ from our own. To express ourselves effectively, we need to gain an insight into the cultural patterns of our listeners, because good communication is much more than the fluent expression of our own ideas: it is about connecting with the understanding of our listeners, at their level. This insight goes far beyond mere linguistic differences. It leads to cultural sensitivity and respect. And it can be learned.

We gained a deep insight one day in Finland. Towards the end of a management development course, we decided to show the group a 10-minute episode from Stephen Covey's video *The Seven Habits of Highly Effective People*. In the clip, Stephen tries to 'motivate' his son to keep their backyard clean. For us this emotionally-charged episode is one where you learn as much about yourself as you do about your child. The Finns were extremely quiet afterwards. Eventually they said it was like an American soap opera. To them it bore no resemblance to how they deal with their children (and by the way, the Finns hate being emotional!). We learned a lesson that day. We were reminded that what might work for us might have no meaning for those from a different culture.

Here's another example: a colleague of ours went to Thailand and was teaching English to a group of 15-year-olds. He decided to get the youngsters to read aloud, individually, around the class. He asked a young girl to be the first reader. She said nothing. He asked her again, and still she said nothing. Knowing that the girl was more than capable of the task, he approached her desk. Immediately she looked down. He asked her again. She remained silent and her head sank even lower. She just wouldn't look at him. The teacher decided that this was an act of defiance, and demanded that the girl stand on her chair and read aloud. The girl ran out of the room sobbing and didn't return for three weeks. Belatedly, our colleague learned a few cultural differences: first, bowing your head (no eye contact) is a sign of respect. Secondly, to be singled out from the crowd is very uncomfortable for people who have been brought up not to 'show off as individuals'. Thirdly, he had asked a girl!

UNLOCKING THE GATES

There are keys to unlocking the gates of cultural understanding. These are focused on people's attitudes to:

◆ status, respect and equality
◆ time, rules and regulations
◆ individuality, family and community
◆ learning, knowledge and sharing
◆ security or risk and self-reliance
◆ the environment.

If you understand these issues and learn how other cultures perceive them, your communication will be much more effective.

However much we learn, we can still get it wrong, as one person discovered when he tried to describe skyscrapers to a young Middle-Eastern goatherd. He described them accurately, portrayed their enormity, and could see by the expression on the youngster's face that the 14-year-old boy had understood what he was saying. Then, to his consternation, the child asked him, 'How many goats do you keep in a skyscraper?'.

THE CLUES IN LANGUAGE

Language differences are hugely significant. Language isn't just how people speak – it is who they are. Knowing the language gives you an insight into the people. When you learn the language of another people, you notice differences in structure, vocabulary and shades of meaning, and that helps you to understand their outlook. Thailand has 12 words for 'you', denoting the importance of seniority. An East African tribe has numerous words for green, reflecting the importance to them of nature's many shades. Nepal has different words for 'uncle', according to whether he is the brother of your mother or father, and whether he is older or younger than your parent. French and Hindi both have 'familiar' terms for you/thou, which are used either for intimates such as your family or when speaking down to someone. In French it's *tu/toi*, in Hindi it's *toom*. In both cases, your tone of voice makes the distinction.

One noticeable difference between languages is the direct/indirect or active/passive contrast. The English language, for example, has sayings that reflect an efficient, activist-driven society: 'Actions speak louder than words' and 'Time is money'. The language itself is structured efficiently too: subject – verb – object. German, on the other hand, sets the scene before revealing the verb at the end. Arabs will tend to use the passive voice, e.g. 'It was observed...' instead of 'I observed...' In each case, the national characteristics are revealed in the structure of their language. Those attitudes are carried over into the way they use English, even if they do not translate directly from their language into English.

When we have run business writing training courses for Arabs, for example, we have had to take account of their reluctance to use the active voice or to be direct. And in our courses on cross-cultural communication, we have to vary the examples we use for illustration, according to the nationalities of the delegates. Northern Europeans may quickly notice something odd about a certain dialogue, but South Americans may not, because what jars on the former may be quite normal for the latter. The significance, however, isn't just the linguistic differences, but rather the attitudes that lie behind them, and the cultural values that give rise to those attitudes.

HOW TO BRIDGE THE GAP

Can you remember the last time you spoke to a foreigner whose English was limited? Perhaps instinctively you limited your vocabulary, slowed down your pace and even used hand gestures to a much greater extent. If that's what you did, you could be a good communicator. The trick is to modify your use of English in a way that works well in all such situations.

Let's remind ourselves of the characteristics of English speakers that cause the most problems, then either eliminate them or find some alternative. Native speakers of English tend to:

1. speak too fast
2. have unfamiliar regional accents
3. use colloquialisms
4. use metaphors
5. use irony or sarcasm
6. modify or qualify their opinions
7. use non-universal vocabulary
8. muddy the meaning for the sake of politeness.

Too fast
Although most people will normally speak more slowly and deliberately, remember not to put pauses between individual words, but rather between short phrases, to allow the other person time to make a mental translation, and also to store some of your phrases for future use.

Accents
Regional accents make it harder for foreigners to understand you. Even Americans find it difficult to cope with any noticeable English accent. We, in turn, can miss large chunks of Hollywood film dialogue until our ears becomes attuned to the rhythm and pronunciation of a non-standard American voice.

Colloquialisms
In Britain, we pepper our speech with such terms as 'gobsmacked', 'griping', 'I was crackers', 'I turned around and said', 'give and take'. They only baffle a foreigner. Remember that 'Out of sight, out of mind' was once translated into Russian as 'Blind idiot'.

Metaphors
Another cause of confusion is the use of metaphors and similes, such as 'It's not rocket science' and 'Their eyes were out on stalks'. Word pictures are good, but standard English metaphors do not always travel well.

Irony and sarcasm
America is often referred to as 'the land of the irony free' because Americans say what they mean and cannot understand the British tendency to mock and to say the opposite of what they really mean. A Greek tourist was

travelling (the wrong way) on London Underground's Circle Line, and asked an Englishman, 'Does this train go to Liverpool Street?' The Brit replied, 'Eventually.' The Greek laughed at his manner, but completely missed his meaning, and got to his destination the long way round.

Modifying or qualifying

By adding words like 'quite' and 'rather', the English make it hard for foreigners who do not understand the shades of meaning they are intended to convey. Not only that, some words are used to mean very different things in different contexts. 'I did quite well' is a modest way of saying 'I did very well', whereas 'I quite liked the film' means it was only moderately pleasing.

Non-universal vocabulary

Apart from jargon and pretentiously long words, confusion can arise over such phrases as this extract from an article in *The Times*: 'Beckham...can get away with clunking pectoral crosses (and) incorporate a medallion into (his) manly apparatus.'

Excessive politeness

Most people with even a smattering of English will understand 'toilet' but not euphemisms like 'washroom' or 'little boy's room'. Other typical English phrases to avoid are 'I wonder if you'd mind...' and 'Would you like to...'. They have no direct equivalent in other languages, and only muddy your meaning.

So how should you avoid obstacles to clear meaning? The best solution is to be aware of the eight points just listed, and use simple language. In particular:

- Use the active voice, e.g. 'I said this' not 'It was said'.

- Describe exactly what you mean, without fancy images, e.g. 'heavy metal crosses around his neck' not 'clunking pectoral crosses'.

- Say what you mean, in a way that does not leave them guessing, e.g. 'Please come to dinner at the Roma Restaurant, as my guests. It will be my way of repaying your hospitality.'

- Use short sentences, without subordinate clauses. Avoid saying, 'I was glad to see the film was on, which, by the way, I always meant to see when it first came out, except that there was always something that prevented me from ever getting there, and I managed to get in after an early dinner, which I badly needed.'

- Decide exactly what you mean to say and say it – cut out the clutter.

- Use familiar phrases and pause between them, to allow the other person to make a mental translation and take in the meaning of what you said.

- Even with people who are fluent in English, you should start slowly, to allow them to tune their ears to your English accent.

By the year 2020 there will be just three principal languages: Chinese, Spanish and Bad English. You can help make English universally understood, by ensuring you translate your message into the context of your listener and not just your words. Let's not be divided by a common language.

9

Connecting with the Audience

'If we listen to words merely, and give them our own habitual values, we are bound to go astray.'

(Freya Stark, *The Journey's Echo*)

When addressing an audience in any kind of formal way, one of the most important considerations is how they listen, and that could be determined by what they listen for. Of course, each individual has his or her own agenda, but it is always worth taking account of two factors:

1. the reason why you are presenting (and therefore why they are there)

2. national characteristics of the audience (and what is the norm in their country).

The reason for your presentation may mean that:

- the audience is going to compare your proposals with those of a competitor, or

- they may just be expecting information, facts and figures

- they may be expecting inspiration, motivation or enlightenment.

Some nations expect humour at the start, while others positively hate it. However, whatever the circumstances, certain nations listen very differently from others, and it is essential to be aware of what is usual among the people you are addressing. Debbie had a couple of disconcerting experiences in **Finland** before she learned what was going on.

On the first occasion, she was presenting her credentials to a group of Finns, when seeking a training assignment. They sat in respectful silence throughout her presentation, at the end of which she asked, 'Any questions?' There was total silence which, eventually, the chairman broke to ease her embarrassment. Debbie got the assignment, so she never understood what had happened.

A short time later, she made a presentation to another Finnish group. The same thing happened. 'Any questions?' met with total silence. Then someone giggled and said, 'Haven't you realised that we are Finns?'

'What exactly does that mean?' asked Debbie.

'It means,' said the Finn, 'that we don't ask questions because we don't consider it necessary. You are the expert in your subject. You decide what to tell us about it. Why should we ask you questions about something you had decided to leave out? We listen to you and the case you make, and if we like it we may accept it. If not, we listen to someone else and see if we prefer what he has to say.'

Clearly, the Finns have a pretty black and white approach, while other nations like to expand the discussion and maybe make it more specific to themselves. It is therefore vital to adapt your presentation and presenting style to match the listening styles and expectations of your listeners.

HOW WERE THEY TAUGHT TO LEARN?

When we were conducting a programme with some diplomats from **Malawi**, we noticed that they were all diligently scribbling as though they were in a school classroom. We asked why and they replied that it was how they had been taught to learn – to take copious notes which they could later read and digest. There was a cultural influence at work as well, which was to show us respect by taking down our words of wisdom. To sit back and simply listen might imply that they were not very interested in what we had to say. (We had noticed a similar tendency among **Arabs**.)

When we asked how they could listen and understand while writing notes, they were totally nonplussed. They asked, 'Don't you want us to take notes?' We said 'No.' Or rather, 'Write down only those points that you particularly want to remember and use.'

It is virtually impossible for most people to retain anything much if they try to write and listen at the same time, and yet many countries persist in requiring their pupils to do so at school and university. It imposes on the pupil the double task of taking notes in class, then trying to makes sense of them later, when the teacher is not present to explain or fill in any gaps. This is one reason why learning is so slow in those countries, and why there is a gap between what is memorised and what is applied. It's a bit like having the workings of a gearbox explained to you, then getting into a car and having to work out for yourself how and when to change gear.

We described their traditional teaching/learning method as an 'exchange'. The teacher had information to impart, and the pupils received it passively, placing it alongside the information they already had. It was a transaction, like handing over a library book. Useful information, useless method. In contrast, our approach was to create change – in the thinking and practices of our listeners. Useful ideas, immediately usable.

When we explained our (different) approach, they were surprised but delighted. We said we wanted them to understand what we were telling them – not later, but in the here and now. If they understood the message and could relate it to what they already knew and to their working lives, they had a far better chance of changing their way of thinking and of doing things – that very day. Of course, it required us to use techniques that would help them to remember the new ideas, and that brought us to the second cultural change.

We pointed out that effective communication was a two-way street. We didn't want to deliver a series of lectures with questions at the end of each – which is the norm in many countries. Rather, we wanted them to ask questions along the way, and to participate in activities that would enhance their understanding as well as make it easier to remember the new ideas. In answering their questions, we usually started with an idea that they already knew and accepted, and then extended it to embrace the new thinking.

To any Brit or American reading this, our approach might not seem very different from your own experience. Yet it was totally new to the Malawians and Arabs. What's more, when we later tested their recall, it was far higher than even they expected. Among the Arabs it may be because they tend to process information associatively, so they are accustomed to the idea of learning by association. The lesson we learned was that it is possible to replace outdated exchange learning with change learning, despite the conditioning of school days and subsequent education.

However, some countries such as Mexico and Venezuela are beginning to take new initiatives in their drive for better education. Venezuela has created a new cabinet post, 'Minister of State for the Development of Human Intelligence'. The objective is to increase Venezuelan competence in the modern world. The Minister has decided to teach thinking skills, recognising that students in developed countries are taught to think whereas in Venezuela they are taught to memorise and repeat without any creative or analytical effort. A move from exchange to change learning!

GETTING FEEDBACK
Nigerians (and **Koreans**) listen differently. In our experience they are vocal and participative. Ask the group a rhetorical question and they will jump in with the answer! Even an obvious bridging question like, 'So what do we

learn from this?' will be considered an invitation to dialogue and draw from them a peppering of opinions. It can be both encouraging and disconcerting because it is unexpected, but it can lead to a lively exchange. Clearly, they have been influenced by the educational system in their country but, in addition, the Nigerians we have encountered have been extremely willing to learn.

The **Japanese** can pose a real problem for Europeans. One British businessman described them in this way: 'A room full of Japanese businessmen will smile at you politely until you begin your presentation. Then they will drop their chins on to their chests and appear to fall asleep. When you have finished, they will stand and bow, then file out of the room without giving you any feedback. Because of their custom of leaving it to the most senior person to speak, you will never know what any individual in the group thinks about what you have said or presented.'

Traditionally, the Japanese have tended to make their decisions within the group, ignoring outside contributions. They have tended to make those decision based on how they feel about the issue and anyone presenting it, but their judgements have mainly been filtered through their group's self-interest. However, among the younger generation there seems to be a trend towards western-style independence and equality, and their competitiveness makes them more receptive to ideas that will give them the edge.

In making presentations to the Japanese, it is advisable to make few, and only economical, gestures, always avoiding any that suggest mateyness. Never point with your fingers, but push your upturned palm towards the object you are indicating. The Japanese will probably close down on you if you display negative emotion such as irritation or anger, as that would be undignified.

The right buttons to press, when addressing the Japanese are probably those covering teamwork, craftsmanship, consensus and corporate pride. The Japanese language is full of honorifics which imply degrees and kinds of mutual obligations. Remember, too, that increasing numbers of Japanese organisations are setting up in Europe, so more Europeans are having Japanese bosses, and must adapt to Japanese ways of working. One frequent cause of difficulty lies in the Japanese custom of saying 'Yes' (see Chapter 7) to signify, 'I hear' or 'I understand', not 'I agree'. If they nod during your presentation, it is most likely just to encourage you and let you know that they have heard you, nothing more.

MEETING EXPECTATIONS
Communication fails when expectations are not met. Quite commonly, people listen for a confirmation of what they already know or believe. However simple your message and however clearly you put it across, you can be certain someone will totally miss the point because it wasn't what he expected to hear.

In Britain, you can divert your phone calls to another number by dialling *21*, then the number of your choice. Later, you can cancel the divert by dialling #21#. When Debbie first used the system, she forgot how to cancel the divert, so she rang our PA at the office and was given the code: #21#. A little while later she rang again to say it wasn't working. She had repeatedly dialled *21* – that's what she had heard because that's what she expected to hear.

Americans have such a fixation about opening their presentations with a joke that they fret if they cannot be funny. One American was told not to try that in Japan, where they prefer seriousness and humility or even an opening apology. So he started his presentation with an apology for not having a joke to tell!

Peter Legge is Canada's foremost motivational speaker. He uses a lot of humour, possibly because he was once a stand-up comic. He even used to make his wife the butt of his jokes. ('My wife has run off with my best friend…and I miss him!') Their marriage is a strong and secure one, and he knew she didn't mind. However. One day a friend took him aside and said, 'Pete, cut that out. You can't see the pain in her heart.' Of course, she made allowances for him because of their good relationship, but you cannot expect a similar indulgence from your business audiences. The French, for instance, heartily dislike jokes against the family.

On a different level, it is essential to tune in to your audience, whether it happens to be a handful of people sitting round a table, or a conference hall with two or three thousand folks facing you. The opening few seconds are vital. It's the 'sniffing period', just like the meeting of two dogs, when each decides if the other is friend or foe.

An audience judges you as soon as you appear or stand to speak. It is vital to make a connection, establish some commonality, encourage them to feel warm towards you. A dignified but friendly bearing usually works. High energy entrances, like Tony Robbins, should be used only selectively. Northern Europeans and Orientals are likely to be turned off, especially if it is a business meeting, not a motivational seminar.

One of Phillip's more difficult experiences was when a voice coach invited him to share a training half-day, but specified that he would cover all the vocal training, while Phillip covered the presentation skills. On cue, following a couple of hours on vocal variety, Phillip took the stage and launched into the techniques of putting your message together and putting it across. He sensed resistance amongst the delegates, which turned to active hostility. Eventually, the training manager (who was one of the delegates) said, 'This is all about presentation skills. We did that last week. We were expecting voice training today.' Phillip had been given the wrong brief, so it was not his fault, but ever since that day he starts each training day by asking delegates to say what they expect to gain from the day, and he finishes the day by returning to the checklist and asking the delegates if they agree that all objectives have been met.

National attitudes prevail too. Some nations would have been too polite to say, 'We did this last week.' They would have sat and wasted the day. Others would have asked for specific changes to the day's agenda.

UNDERSTANDING ATTITUDES

Individualistic nations (Hispanics, French speakers, Germans) would be prepared to accept that a meeting should move towards an outcome. They will, of course, come with their own proposals, and attempt to impose them on the meeting. Others, such as the Dutch, Irish, Swedes and Italians will be prepared to pool ideas and arrive at a consensus. Arabs may not arrive at any resolution until late in the day, in the car on the way home, when they feel a good rapport has been established with you.

Style

Americans stand at one end of the scale when it comes to the style of speaking. They are easily bored if the speaker is not charismatic. The Brits are similar, but are more tolerant of a poor speaker. Spaniards and Hispanic Americans have a low attention span and you need to be theatrical, while the Italians pay attention only if it concerns or benefits themselves. The French hardly listen at all, but they like eloquence and flowery language, as do the Indians. Arabs will start talking among themselves if the speaker is weak. The Japanese may appear to fall asleep, but they are listening and weighing you up according to how well you present. Germans and Finns want the facts, while the Scandinavians are cynical.

The best advice is to save extremes of performance theatrics for when you know they will be welcome, but always encourage response during your presentation.

Short-term

British and American business is driven by 2–3 year business plans. We value short-term gain and we are always looking for immediate results. Training is regarded as a 'quick fix'. Typically, the managing director of a City business will phone a training organisation and say, 'I have a major presentation to deliver in a couple of weeks. Book me in for a two-hour session on Friday to sharpen up my skills.' He will then expect a total transformation in that session.

The rest of Europe has a longer term focus – especially the Finns and the Swedes. Training courses in Europe are longer – they appreciate it will take time to develop a skill. Similarly, in selling, the phrase 'closing the sale' reveals the underlying obsession with short-term gain. Get the sale now, get the deal done now, and move on. However, the Eastern mentality would prefer to take time to open and develop the relationship. This should guide your proposals, and the time frame you envisage.

Long-term

It's not unusual for a Japanese business to have a 50-year business plan. At least one major organisation boasts of a 250-year plan! When you take the long view, you can bear short-term losses to establish a secure base for the future. To enter the Japanese market you may need to spend five years getting to know people and establishing relationships before you can do any business. Countries in Latin America and Asia are all longer term focused. Even in the 'hurry-up' West, business thinking is moving towards relationship marketing, in which suppliers aim to be proactive in meeting the needs of their clients or customers, standing shoulder to shoulder and solving problems rather than selling boxes of hardware.

It is generally better to propose a cautious time frame and allow your audience to ask for something quicker.

Deadlines

Typical phrases in western vocabulary are 'clock watching', 'time is money', 'waste time', 'spend time', 'save time' and so on, all denoting a fixation with deadlines and the efficient use of time. Few other nations speak about time as a commodity. We break time and tasks into chunks in order to schedule and programme them. High value is placed on punctuality, efficiency, and progress. It is a characteristic of English speaking nations and northern Europeans, and Americans seem to believe that it is possible to control time.

The governing factor is not to focus too much attention on deadlines and efficiency when relationship building (which takes time) is more important to your audience.

Deference

In the West, the age of deference has gone. The boss is no longer always right, and no one ever says, 'Yes sir, no sir, three bags full, Sir.' In fact, hardly anyone says Sir any more. Increasingly, especially in Britain and America, everyone is called by their first names. Not so in the East. East of India, the norm is to be respectful listeners. People still defer to their seniors and will tend to say what they think their superiors want to hear. They will also avoid saying anything that might offend. This attitude of deference needs to be understood and applied (if necessary). Remember the key word here is *respect* – be very respectful of your audience.

Pace

Westerners are always in a hurry. Projects have time budgets as well as financial ones. As soon as A is complete, B must follow. Then it must be C. There is no reason for a delay in between. Proposals and presentations are made briskly, and their implementation follows the same pattern. South and east of the Mediterranean, however, it is very different. Africans dislike rapid presentations. They prefer things to move slowly and smoothly, and they like to be warmed up like friends. They like to be liked. Indians take things at a very measured pace, and they have perfected the art of bureaucratic blocking. Push too hard and you'll find yourself having to go through endless hoops.

Past

For some nations, the past is everything – it's where you come from and who you are. The French prefer the *Ancien Pauvre* to the *Nouveau Riche*, and they like to place initiatives in the context of the past. The Brits look at whether a proposal fits into the existing plan and established patterns. In the Far East, an American factory manager told his staff he was going to make a new start and turn things round, getting rid of old practices. He was baffled by the rumble of discontent. He did not realise that he was giving insult to ancestors, whose continued influence was revered by the staff. In their culture, everything in the past influences our present and future.

Present

Some languages and cultures are very present-oriented. Philippine society will enjoy today, spend all their money today, cannot conceive of planning for tomorrow. Their thinking is shaped by their different sense of time and by their method of education, which to learn by heart or by rote. This means they cannot easily handle abstract thinking, and they will tend to cling to the familiar in the here and now.

Future

Western nations have a diminishing interest in the past. The past is past. We can make our own future. Our language includes such phrases as 'clean sweep', 'clean break', 'new broom'. Americans believe good planning will enable them to forecast and be in control of the future – it's what they call progress and achievement. The Arabic language, in contrast, has only tenuous linguistic structures for talking about the future. In their view, the future is in the hands of Allah.

Cycles

Traditional Buddhist culture treats time and one's personal involvement with it as evolving cycles rather than as a linear progression. This is so alien to Western thinking that it is hard for us to contemplate, so we usually ignore its implications! We believe in cause and effect, whereas Buddhist thinking urges us to accept that periods of low fortune will be replaced by better ones...eventually. In the West we want to make things happen, and bring about change through our own efforts. In the East they accept that *what will be will be*.

Emotion: expressed

Nations that prefer to show how they feel expect others to exhibit anger, joy or any other emotion openly and honestly, and feel uneasy with those who do not do so.

Southern Europe and Latin America are highly expressive, verbally and non-verbally. In negotiations they might bang their fists on tables, showing displeasure. To them that is normal, not excessively aggressive. To the Japanese, Americans can seem quite uncontrolled and socially incompetent when they get carried away with enthusiasm or make an argument with feeling. Conversely, the Japanese confuse Americans with their restrained emotions and responses which do not signal inner feelings.

Emotion: checked

Some nations prefer to avoid expressing emotion openly. To them it is unseemly to display joy, anger or disappointment within normal relationships. They are reserved and expect others to be the same. For them the open expression of emotion is uncomfortable for others, and embarrassing. The Japanese and Chinese have inscrutable faces; the UK has stiff upper lips; Finns seem as cold as their frozen lakes; Scandinavians and Germans do not allow emotion to play a part in business. These are, of course, generalisations based on historical norms and even stereotypes. However, it would be foolhardy to ignore them.

What really matters is not to create a different approach for each national type, because you will end up trying to cope with 27 different versions of your message. Rather, it would be wise to consider a universal approach, such as the 4C model, which incorporates such common sense elements as respect, a clear map of your message, and a balanced mixture of factual content and emotional appeal, leading to a clearly signposted outcome.

In our experience, every nation responds to being addressed as individuals, not as a mass. It is never advisable to throw scripts at the audience, but rather to deliver the message as though to each person individually. That's the general advice. Of course, certain audiences respond to a 'performance', and that is worth delivering. But it is not a universal preference.

In summary, then, you should start by asking yourself:

- What do I want at the end of this presentation?
- Why are they coming?
- What are their expectations?
- Why should they listen to me?
- How do they listen?
- How can I shape my message to their understanding?

It will help to condition your thinking, so that your opening few seconds allow you to connect with them and persuade them to start listening to you.

10

Making an International Presentation

'No two languages are ever sufficiently similar to be considered as representing the same social reality. The worlds in which different societies live are distinct, not merely the same world with different labels attached.'

(Edward Sapir:
Culture, Language and Personality)

Through our training company, 4C International Ltd, we have worked in a number of countries all around the world, as well as with UK companies that do business in foreign markets. We noticed a great disparity of standards in the presentations we saw – in their:

◆ content
◆ reasoning
◆ style
◆ delivery
◆ cross-cultural relevance.

In some places, the venerable overhead projector (OHP) still has pride of place! It brought home to us that it is not safe to assume that all nations have progressed at a uniform rate. Nor are their expectations all the same. In general, the standards abroad were far lower than in Britain and the United States, and in some places they had been taught presentation techniques by trainers who were years out of date. Also, the presentations often seemed to have been prepared in the local language, then translated directly into English. Inevitably they were stilted and convoluted, and they just did not work.

To native speakers of English and those whose international experience has given them fluency in the English language and the Anglo-American way of presenting a persuasive argument, the unsophisticated presentations of some nations are frankly boring.

Fairly typical of many presentations was one by a Finnish company that began with a map of their location (within Finland) and a picture of their factory. Next came a declaration of their credentials – a compendium of their products and processes. Even before they got to anything relevant to their audience they had lost the interest of all but the Finns in the audience.

At a recent Russian conference, several presentations committed several elementary errors. There were too many slides, they were packed with too many words, the type was too small to read from a distance, there were lots of slides of pages copied from books, and there were masses of figures which were impossible to take in. 'Look at these figures!' the presenter would say, pointing at the screen that no one could read.

Turning to British and American presentations, we noticed that most tended to make no allowances for the cultural differences of their foreign audiences, apart from a few token gestures towards known customs. In this chapter therefore, we shall offer our suggestions for the kind of presentation that might have the widest appeal – in any country, just as long as the language used is English.

English is pretty much the universal business language, but as we have mentioned earlier in the book, international English is more direct and less colloquial than the day-to-day language used in Britain. Nevertheless, the presentation style we have developed for our international training programmes is based on the Anglo-Saxon approach, especially in:

♦ structure
♦ development of the argument
♦ mixture of facts and emotional appeal
♦ style of the visual aids
♦ techniques of delivery.

In international presentations, whether delivered in Britain or abroad, it is essential to bridge the 'comprehension gap'. This can arise because the presenter is speaking too fast, or is using unfamiliar vocabulary (including the misuse of familiar words), or has a reasoning process that is hard to follow. Once this comprehension gap occurs, those in the audience will stop listening and become preoccupied with questions in their own minds, such as 'What are you saying? Where are you going with this? Why did you use that word in that context?' Pretty soon those questions give way to hostile statements (in the mind) like, 'I don't agree with that' and 'I wish you'd stop'.

In the previous chapter we dealt with connecting with the audience. Here we shall deal with ways to prevent such negative reactions in the first place.

CONTENT

Let's start with the basics. Whenever we ask people how many parts there are in a presentation, they say 'Three: beginning, middle and end.' So let's accept that, and consider what kind of shape the presentation should take, within that outline. But let's call the three stages A, B and C (Approach, Body and Conclusion).

There are two main types of content: factual and emotional, and you should consider the right mix in each of the three stages of the presentation. If we were to draw it as a grid, it would look like this:

	A	B	C
Factual			
Emotional			

Germans, Finns and Norwegians have no time for small talk or warming up, and they like their factual content to start almost from the opening sentence, and run through to the very end. So their grid would have the upper (factual) level fully shaded, with little or nothing at the bottom (emotional) level.

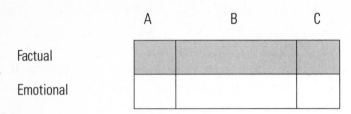

	A	B	C
Factual			
Emotional			

Americans, on the other hand, like to start with a bang, move on to humour, take the emotions on a roller coaster ride, and go out on a Wow! So their grid would have the bottom level full, with perhaps a tiny bit of factual content in the middle of the body.

	A	B	C
Factual			
Emotional			

Clearly, it's no good giving an American-style presentation to a German audience, or vice versa.

The pattern we recommend is a balance between the two. In simple terms, it works like this:

1. Start with a **hook** to connect with the audience. The hook could be a surprising fact or statistic, and should be dramatic enough to grab attention, while being relevant to the audience and the occasion.

2. Follow that up with a **map** – not the location of your firm, but an outline of your presentation, indicating

what you will be covering and in what order. Everyone likes to know where you will be taking them.

3. Follow a clear **structure**. Not only will it keep you on track, but your listeners will find it easier to follow you and understand how each point relates to all the others you are making.

4. When you make a statement or a claim, **back it up** with the facts or source. The French, for example, will always want to know. Then answer the question, 'So what?' and explain why the point is significant and how it relates to your theme.

5. Every time you **conclude a section** of your presentation, or a specific argument, make it clear that you are about to move on to the next point: e.g. 'So much for the historical background. Let me now turn to the present day, and show how our current problems have resulted directly from what happened in the past.'

6. Think of each point you make as a **building brick**, and place one on top of another to form a towering structure that people can see and admire, and understand what it is for. Don't just place the bricks side by side or you will end up with a pile of bricks that mean nothing. Multicultural audiences need to know the plan and see how and why each brick is placed where it goes, and then they need to be reassured that they are seeing the completed structure correctly.

7. Let your arguments lead to a **logical conclusion** – one that allows your audience the chance to buy into your thinking (see the completed structure) and accept your proposition.

8. Plan your **opening and closing sentences** with equal precision and care. Those are the words they will best remember.

These guidelines may be universally applicable, but they are especially helpful in addressing international audiences, and have been compiled from our own multicultural experiences.

REASONING

Be aware that not all nations process information the same way. The Russians, French and Italians tend to be **deductive** and to focus on specific instances. They do not like being given a general principle and being left to decide how and if it applies to them. They like to be told, and to have it proved. They listen for the word 'Because...'.

Others listen only to what you are saying at that moment, and they carry no baggage. They will not retain each element of the argument until you finally reveal the inevitable conclusion! Instead, they will be prepared to go along with you for as long as you enable them to feel good about you and what you are saying – they will give you an emotional acceptance at each point of resolution. It's **relationship building**, as far as they are concerned, and they need not be pressed to agree with the facts or the reasoning. In such cases, it is your demeanour and personal credibility that count more than the content of your presentation.

STYLE

The style of your presentation includes the professional-ism of your audio-visual aids and how you use them, your support material, and your personal appearance.

It is always best to aim high and expect your audience to have the highest standards, even if they don't. The use of a short video and music at the start is unusual and memorable, so long as it is relevant. The use of an OHP, on the other hand, might signal 'old fashioned' or 'unsophisticated', unless there is nothing else available. PowerPoint may not be everyone's favourite, but it can provide a very effective solution if it is not overdone.

Three general pieces of advice concerning visual aids: use props and anything that is visual, but not too many slides, and keep the words on each slide to a minimum. Let the visual aids support but not supplant you and your message. Making it visual will help to overcome the language barrier. Pictures do not require translation.

DELIVERY

Most nations enjoy a **performance**, but it should not be overdone. Apart from North America and Britain, few nations like a business presentation to be theatrical, or they will think you are treating it like a game. Balance emotion and fact. Someone once wrote:

> 'Reason is cold, but it sees clearly. Give it warmth but do not cloud its clarity.'

That said, vocal variety and direct connection with the audience will always add a positive dimension to the presentation. So make it a performance but not a 'performance'. If you are using figures and statistics, translate them into graphics and always show them in comparison with something else, such as the previous year's figures. Then go the extra step and interpret them. Don't leave your audience to work out if it is good, bad or indifferent.

In countries where public speaking has not progressed much beyond the academic arena, presenters will tend to stand behind lecterns and deliver lectures. These are not much more than scripts hurled at the audience, and are as ineffective as they are boring. One might as well deliver the message by email. If you are presenting in person you should add your personal conviction to the message, but vary its intensity according to how far north you are at the time. Be cool but definite in the north, but let your passion flow freely where the climate's sultry.

CROSS-CULTURAL RELEVANCE

As we stated at the start of this chapter, too many presentations to international audiences neglect to take account of the needs and expectations of their listeners. It is always worth remembering that most advanced nations prefer their own solutions (and local solution providers), unless they do not have them at home. Their starting position is likely to be, 'Why should we turn to you – someone who does not know our market, our lifestyle, our circumstance?' That view will only be reinforced if your approach is the same as if you were addressing a domestic audience.

At the same time, it would be worth reversing the process, and developing an international approach that you apply in your domestic market as well, because you have cross-cultural staff and cross-cultural customers at home already.

Finally, some general words of advice. The techniques and disciplines of good presentations in Britain and the US will generally be relevant throughout the world, especially if the US enthusiasm is leavened with a substantial portion of fact. In addition, treat every presentation as a persuasive communication, and treat every audience with the respect you would give to the elderly head of a major Japanese corporation.

11

Tips on Communicating with Different Nations

'The embracing of culture in all its diversity as a resource rather than a threat is essential for responding to the demands of a global market economy, for reaping the full benefit of cross-border alliances, and for enhancing organizational learning.'

(Schneider and Barsoux,
Managing Across Cultures)

All cultures use a mix of written, oral and visual communication, but some tend to have a bias towards one or another. In Europe there is a broad sweep of preference for written or literal communication across the northern countries, while the southern countries prefer oral communication. There is a similar East/West distinction, with the West generally favouring written communication, as in contracts and orders, while the East works on oral agreements.

Here are three general guidelines to make your communication more effective:

1. People from more literal cultures do not accept spoken words as total commitment unless they are

confirmed in writing. It is advisable to follow up telephone conversations with a letter, fax or email.

2. People from more oral cultures may regard written confirmations merely as a simple record and give it no more attention. Indeed, it is a good idea to follow up a letter or email with a phone call, if only to confirm that the correspondence has been received and read.

3. In North America communication is primarily literal (strongly email), but is much more visual than in Europe, with widespread use of graphics, diagrams, and logos.

Let's consider the preferences in certain European countries.

FINLAND

- ◆ The Finns are one of the most honest people in the world.

- ◆ They are even more direct than Norwegians, but not rude.

- ◆ They are not interested in small talk or developing relationships, so get to the point.

- ◆ They prefer written communication, to make appointments or to confirm agreements.

- ◆ Their letters and emails are written in peremptory terms that read like demands.

- ◆ They have a sense of humour, even against themselves.

- ◆ Finns are very shrewd and models of efficiency.

- They are quick to decide…and to implement.

- However, they are poor at marketing themselves.

- They expect the facts (and their products) to speak for themselves.

FRANCE

- Writing letters and emails, and even minutes of meetings, is considered a waste of time. The French prefer to make phone calls for that kind of communication.

- For formal reporting, the French give high marks to clear, well-structured reports that are well written and cogently argued. They respect the linguistic skill as much as the content.

- Business relationships are conducted in a professional and serious manner, but there is always an under-current of personal networking that gets things done. It is impossible to be successful in France without developing relationships based on intellectual respect.

- Informal, off-the-record contacts are very important.

- Your use of the French language, both spoken and written, must be correct. They do not lightly forgive poorly written letters.

- Unlike the Anglo Saxons, the French do not write colloquially. The quality of language is a mark of education and professionalism.

GERMANY

- Germans are not good on the phone. They use no preamble and get straight to the point.

- They are inhibited, especially on a conference call.

- They duplicate everything: face-to-face meetings are confirmed in writing – in detail.

- They like everything written down, and scrutinise it for accuracy.

- Communication with the Germans is on a need-to-know basis. They like to get on with the job, and are intolerant of anything that wastes their time.

GREECE

- Oral communication, either face to face or on the phone, is most important.

- Phone conversations can be very lengthy and involve personal relationships.

- Letters and emails can be very formal, as written communications are not the norm.

- Written communications, especially confirmations of verbal agreements, can make the recipients anxious.

ITALY

- Italians enjoy the process of communication more than its purpose. They like to talk and need to be allowed the time and space to do so.

- Personal relationships are vital, both when you need information and when you need to get something done.

- They favour face-to-face meetings, and the telephone more than the mail.

- They like phone calls to prepare the ground before meetings.

- Informal contacts are important, and they like being on the inside track, with the right connection.

NORWAY

- The Norwegians are similar to the Swedes, but have a better sense of humour.

- They prefer written communication, and are happy to deal through emails.

- Their honesty is impeccable.

- They can be very direct, even brutal, when they do not wish to proceed with something.

- In business, they are very approachable, but do not waste their time.

RUSSIA

- A very bureaucratic nation.

- Russians insist on formal procedures such as minutes, notes and action plans (which they call 'protocols'), to clarify and confirm agreements.

- They use business English, but they may not always use the words as you understand them, especially on technical or financial matters.

- They are accustomed to being 'on duty' during all waking hours, and do not hesitate to make late night calls to discuss business matters with colleagues.

SPAIN

- The Spanish preference is for face-to-face oral communication.

- Correspondence and written confirmations are for the largest companies only. Their preference is for a formal but flowery style, using correct titles.

- Write in English unless your command of idiomatic Spanish is perfect, as the risk is great of giving offence through the use of incorrect terms.

- Honour and trust play a big part in their oral agreements.

- They like imagery: flowery language, visual aids, PowerPoint and lots of information.

- Presentations should be conservative and respectful, respecting 'seniority'.

- Present a united front as a team: contradictions indicate weakness and poor preparation.

- If they seem restrained, they are only being courteous and composed.

- Their negotiations are noisy, with raised voices and many interruptions. Don't take offence.

SWEDEN

- Business relationships are kept separate from personal ones.

- Bringing personal matters into a business context is regarded as an intrusion.

- The Swedes guard their personal space.

- Written communication is preferred to spoken, and the Swedes like to follow a formal and structured approach.

- Swedes have excellent English and choose that language for their international dealings.

- They have a democratic, even collective, approach to decision making.

COMMUNICATING EFFECTIVELY IN MEETINGS
First, some international thumbnails on humour:

- Germans dislike humour in serious business situations.

- Finns don't go in for small talk or jokes in a business context, although they will readily tell jokes against themselves over a drink in the bar.

- The Japanese react badly to jokes in a business context, and consider that they indicate a lack of respect for the situation and those present.

- The French enjoy playing with language, admire those who can make linguistic jokes in French, and have a sophisticated sense of humour.

- British humour is too subtle for many foreigners, and the spoken language is full of metaphors, similes and irony.

- America is known (in Britain) as the land of the irony free. Although Americans use humour, they do so ritualistically and do not have a good sense of humour.

◆ The Indians like humour and respond well to it. They like linguistic jokes and puns, and enjoy poking fun at the extreme characteristics of different Indian groups.

There are many reasons why we misunderstand each other. However, here are three significant facts that point to a particular cause, especially in meetings.

1. We think at 500–800 words per minute.

2. We can hear words at about 400 words per minute, even if we record someone's voice and play it back at high speed later.

3. We speak, on average, at about 150 words per minute.

That means we can listen to someone speaking in a presentation or at a meeting, and still have space for our minds to be occupied with something else. It means that we listen actively for only 20–30 per cent of the time. It means that others actively listen to us only 20–30 per cent of the time. The rest of the time is spent either thinking about something else or working out what we mean by what we are saying.

The potential for misunderstanding is therefore great, and we need to ensure that we build into our presentations frequent reminders of what we have said and where we are heading.

MEETINGS IN DIFFERENT CULTURES
First, some general tips on greetings:

- Greet Indians (especially Hindus) with *Namaste*: palms together, chest high, with a slight bow.

- Greet Muslims (especially in the Middle East) with *Salaam Aleikum*, sweeping the right hand towards the heart and forehead.

- Do not offer to shake hands with a Muslim woman: unrelated men are forbidden to touch them.

- In central Europe and part of Scandinavia, nod your head in respect when shaking hands, as though you were going to deliver a head butt.

- The Finns shake hands firmly throughout the business of exchanging introductions.

- The French shake hands all the time, sometimes also kissing on the cheek (either gender).

- In Mediterranean countries the handshake may be accompanied by an arm squeeze.

- The Japanese bow. The greater the respect, the deeper the bow.

The best advice is to watch and copy. You could also ask. It's all right to say, 'In my country we usually shake hands. What do you do in your country?'

Here is how different cultures view meetings, and how they function within them.

FINLAND
- Finns like meetings in order to thrash out problems, plan courses of action, and share ideas and information.

- Punctuality is important, so always arrive on time.

- Despite meticulous preparation, business is seldom completed, because everyone at the meeting is allowed their say.

- The exception is board meetings, which are used to give formal agreement to decisions that may have been made elsewhere.

- Finns are decisive and move quickly to implement their decisions.

- They are literal-minded and answer only the question asked, even if it's not the answer required.

- They will give each other a full hearing, but do not usually ask for elaboration.

FRANCE

- The French respect authority – if it is backed by competence.

- Their meetings follow an established format with a detailed agenda.

- They like the use of honorifics, e.g. *Monsieur, Madame, Professeur, etc.*

- The discussions are about process not outcome, so don't expect decisions or action plans.

- The timetable is a moveable feast, with interruptions and alterations throughout.

- They may agree procedures in a meeting but disregard them later.

- The focus is on establishing relationships first, before getting on with the tasks.

- Business lunches are normally 2–3 hours.

GERMANY

- The Germans like plenty of notice of a meeting.

- They like the agenda and timetable to be fixed and they dislike changes.

- They follow the agenda strictly, and minute everything.

- The meeting will be dominated by the senior person present.

- Major decisions will have been taken before the meeting by the relevant experts.

- Any proposition will have to be presented in precise detail, backed by factual evidence.

- Levity is frowned on.

- They communicate in a very direct way that may sound rude.

GREECE

- Meetings are considered forums for the expression of personal opinions.

- Everyone must have their say.

- Formal agendas are rare.

- Formal minutes are not usually taken, although individuals may take notes.

ITALY

- Italians are undisciplined, even in business.

- Meetings are mainly for the decision makers to receive input from others, for decisions to be made elsewhere.

- Meetings are unstructured and informal, more a social gathering than a business forum.

- Everyone defers to those in authority, and those in authority think they have all the answers.

- It is normal to have long discussions on side issues, so it is advisable to prepare and circulate an agenda in advance.

- Italians over-analyse and split hairs – *spaccare il capello in quattro.*

- For the best chance of getting support for a formal proposal, it is advisable to speak to each participant individually in advance.

JAPAN

- The Japanese respect seniority.

- Long service and grey hair are signs of seniority.

- They enter a meeting room in order of seniority.

- The most senior person sits at the furthest part of the room.

- The Japanese respect silence. It signifies that serious work is being done.

- They do not say 'No' directly, as that is impolite. Therefore it may be necessary to phrase questions in such a way as to ascertain exactly what they intend to do.

- In instructing Japanese, you should be very structured and ensure that they are following every step. They would be offended at any suggestion that they have not understood.

SPAIN

- The Spanish hold meetings to impart decisions and instructions.

- They are undisciplined about the agenda and time-table.

- They need a strong chairperson to keep the discussion on track.

- Spanish organisations are very hierarchical.

- If you are calling a meeting, you should notify senior management, who will then cascade the information downwards to their subordinates.

- Seniority matters, and participants will defer to the boss.

USA

- Americans are very focused and efficient.

- Meetings are for well-defined purposes, and should have action plans at the end.

- They like clear agendas and stick to them.

- They believe in background preparation.

- They speak with passion and make their positions clear.

- They believe that time is money, and don't like to waste any.

- They created the business breakfasts and lunches.

FINALLY...
Cultural differences exist everywhere, and it is futile to try to remember the right protocols for every situation. The quick references above will prepare you to handle responses that are different from those in your own backyard. Just remember the one word, 'respect'. Filter all differences though that word and you will avoid giving offence, even if you make a mistake.

PART 2
Quick Reference Guide for Busy People

12

The Seven Relationship Danger Points of Business

'We are all leaders. Each one of us is setting an example for someone else, and each one of us has a responsibility to shape the future as we wish it to be.'

(A Higher Standard of Leadership: Lessons from the Life of Gandhi)

This book is primarily about doing business internationally – in the English language. It is not about learning how different nations communicate in their own languages, but rather how they use English – international English.

It helps us to understand other cultures when we see how they process information and express their thoughts in English, a language that is very different from many others. For example, the standard English construction is Subject – Verb – Object. I need it. The French, on the other hand, might say, *J'en ai besoin* (I of it have need). It's a very different way of developing their communication. Such differences are more than structural. They reflect mental processes that are quite dissimilar. These differences are even more marked in the idiomatic language, so that direct translations seldom work. We will better understand how other nations think if we examine the way they use language (remember the example of 'Out of sight, out of mind' being translated into Russian as 'Blind idiot'?)

To do business in the global village, we must have the vision and the flexibility to expect and cope with cultural diversity. In our experience of working in a number of countries, East and West, the greatest obstacle is not the lack of a common verbal vocabulary, but rather a reluctance or unwillingness to meet the other person halfway. Companies set on global expansion will be inhibited, and even blocked, if their own people are locked into parochial mindsets. If people believe that only their way is best, if they cannot or will not see merit in diversity, their horizons will remain low, and they will not be able to construct working alliances with those from other cultures. It is preferable to build on what exists, than to force-feed a foreign process.

So let us turn our attention to the seven areas in which poor or mis-communication can undermine a company's international aims. We call them the seven danger points:

1. international meetings
2. international negotiations
3. contracts
4. managing across cultures
5. selling on an international stage
6. living in a politically incorrect world
7. how things get done (bribery and corruption).

These are danger points because they are the areas in

which significant communication takes place, and in which cultural insensitivity can ruin the relationship.

This section will inevitably overlap some of the subject matter of earlier chapters, so that you do not have to constantly refer back to those chapters. In a way, this section aims to take you to the next step, which is to consider how to apply your understanding of cultural differences and their impact on business communication.

INTERNATIONAL MEETINGS

'The hardest thing to get in Europe is simplicity, people saying what they think and feel, openly and directly. It never happens.'

(Stuart Miller, *Understanding Europeans*)

More and more people in all functions and at all levels of organisations are working with foreign colleagues. It is a serious mistake to assume that because we have common interests with other nationalities (and we are speaking a common language – English) we have common ways of achieving our goals. Even among our closest neighbours there are major differences in the way business is conducted and these differences particularly show up during meetings.

Most international meetings are conducted according to 'Western' conventions which allow everyone to **participate equally and fairly** in the meeting, whether it is conducted entirely in English, or in many languages using interpreters.

However, it is amazing that any agreement is ever reached because we will come together with **very different expectations** concerning **every aspect** of the meeting. For example, we believe that those who attend a meeting share a common interest, and perhaps are even focused on the same purpose. In fact, that may not be so.

For a successful meeting we must first recognise that we are conducting ourselves according to our own norms, and that the norms in other countries and other cultures may be very different from ours. Our norms of behaviour may even be considered rude or stupid by others. The important thing is to keep our minds open to differences, and to learn what is acceptable to others, so that effective communication is possible.

Rather than give you stereotypical information on how the French behave, what the Americans will do, or when the Mexicans will turn up, we have collated a checklist of cultural differences for you to consider. Decide what is 'normal' for you, then recognise that your foreign counterparts might think all the other items are normal for them.

Variations due to cultural differences:

What is the purpose and scope of a meeting?
- It is an essential ingredient in getting things done.
- To create an action plan and allocate responsibilities.
- To achieve a definable result and concrete actions.
- To pool information and problem-solve.
- To find opportunities and solutions.

or/and

- Only to brief others with information.
- Just to sanction informal discussions that have taken place elsewhere.
- For mutual understanding and reaffirmation of co-operation.
- For informal networking.
- Taking part and being there is important.
- To create intangible outcomes and sense of direction.

Convention
- Do they start and finish on time?
- Is there a formal agenda?
- There are well-defined roles to control agenda and discussion.
- Contributions are made through the chair when invited.
- Mechanistic approach, process driven.
- Plans are working hypotheses to be negotiated or amended.
- Contributions and challenges are welcomed.

or/and

- Come armed with detailed plan to impose on others.
- Free-for-all, no formalities.
- Lots of breaks for informal group discussion.
- What happens away from the table is more important than what happens at the table.
- Relationship building.

Who will be there?
- The titular head (or trusted deputy).
- Appropriate expert(s).

- Everyone necessary to achieve desired outcome.
- Those who would feel insecure if left out.
- May be unpredictable.
- Are the numbers manageable?

Attitudes to trust

Trust is not a cultural trait, it is a behavioural one: 'a perceived notion regarding a partner's likely behaviour'. Trust is a function of goodwill. Either it is:

- earned, or
- readily given.

Withdrawal only happens when that trust has been 'betrayed'.

Attitudes to agreement

- Adoption of the best idea (hopefully their own!).
- Genuine synthesis.
- Give assent but won't abide by it.
- Full commitment to carrying out whatever agreed at the meeting.

How do you get your own way?

- By motivating people into action.
- By persuasion.
- By exerting your authority (autocratic).
- By influencing: Asian culture prefers to find harmony.

Communication styles

- **Implied**: shared understanding/empathy. It preserves group harmony and avoids embarrassment. Uses voice tone, body language, facial expressions and eye contact.

- **Stated**: explicit statement of what we want or mean.

- **Circular**: need to provide lots of context before answering the question. Indirect.

- **Linear**: provides only the literal answer to the question, without any extra information. Succinct and focused communication.

- **Expressive**: the language is an art form with eloquence and style. Communication is less precise and there is a large emotional content.

- **Instrumental**: the language is a vehicle to communicate ideas. Communication is problem-centred, practical and impersonal.

Who enters first?
- Senior people and heads of delegations always walk in first.
- Seniors come in last.
- It really doesn't matter how people come in.

Seating arrangements
Seating arrangements can make or break a relationship so be careful to prepare properly and do your homework on the cultures you may be hosting. When visiting someone else, be aware that hierarchy systems are often in place, so wait to be shown to your seat. In the Far East, the most senior person sits farthest from the door (often facing it).

Other etiquette to consider
- In some countries a detailed list is required in advance of:
  - objectives you wish to meet
  - each participant's name.

- In many countries only the most senior person does the speaking.

- Don't interrupt when someone from the Far East is speaking; (contrast this with the Italians and US).

- Koreans and Nigerians will interrupt – a desirable sign of eagerness.

- Send someone of 50+ to head your team to countries other than 'western' where seniority, not competence counts.

- Middle East – expect frequent interruptions and for the meeting to be reconvened several times. Often, they even double book.

- Be aware that Muslims pray five times a day and all work ceases then.

How and when to offer your business card
If you have a unique or difficult name to pronounce or remember, offer your name slowly and clearly, repeating it as you hand them your business card, for example, 'I'm Phillip Khan-Panni. Phillip ... Khan ... Panni. Most people, even in Britain, have difficulty pronouncing or spelling that name, so it's useful to see it written down.' This way you are seen to be helping those you meet, rather than pushing your card onto them.

Note: the following comments about exchanging business cards should be considered:

- In the **Middle East** only senior business people exchange cards.

- *Meishi koukan* (business card exchange) is an important part of the **Japanese** business culture.

- In **Asia**, offering and receiving cards is a formal ceremony, filled with respect. Never casually offer your card with just one hand. Hold your card with both hands when you give it and bow slightly.

- It's a courtesy to pass it so that the other person can read it immediately.

- Show respect when you receive a card by using both hands. Look at it, study it, then put it away carefully, like a treasured possession – never in your back pocket!

- Place the card on the table in front of you as an additional sign of respect.

- Don't write on the cards you've just been handed.

- Titles are very important in Asia. They signify seniority and status. However, job titles are being phased out in the US and UK.

Cross-cultural noise
In the **UK** and the **US** meetings always start with a little small talk. Business people in **Europe** and **Latin America** pride themselves on their eloquence and erudition; topics such as philosophy, art, literature, and history will be interwoven with business talk. The **French** like politics, whilst the **Finns** are very educated and take a great interest in economics and world affairs – but in business get straight to the point! Old communist block countries still refer to the 'intelligentsia'.

As you would expect, United Nations debates reflect the variations mentioned above. The 'Anglo Saxons' want to get on with the action and cannot bear all the wrangling over the precise wording of resolutions and other agenda items. Latin nations, and even the Russians, on the other hand, consider it vital to define what has to be discussed before embarking on the debate.

Don't be surprised if the minutes of your meeting don't turn up for nearly a year if you are not responsible for them. A diplomatic acquaintance of ours told us about her time in Nicaragua; over a period of about three years her organisation was always chasing the Nicaraguans for minutes of their meetings until a point was reached when they began to arrive with the minutes already written!

INTERNATIONAL NEGOTIATIONS

'...domestic business dealings probably have about the same relationship to international business as domestic politics do to international diplomacy.'

(Jeswald Salacluse,
*Making Deals in Strange Places; A Beginner's
Guide to International Business Negotiations*)

Five fundamental misconceptions of international negotiations which create false expectations

1. International deals will happen automatically if the correct government policies and structures are in place.

2. The successful strategies and tactics we use in meetings and negotiating at home can apply to international settings.

3. Others' perceptions and stereotyping of us won't be allowed to affect the negotiations.

4. Everyone likes to get down to business and focus on the end game: to achieve a legally binding contract.

5. The 'rules of engagement' are the same all over the world.

Ten distinctive features of international negotiations

1. **Cultural differences** which go beyond language: values, perceptions, beliefs, philosophy and trust. Ideas can mean different things to different nations.

2. **Different ideologies** concerning the purpose of commerce, individual rights, the common good, profit, private investment and government interventions. Successful negotiators will present their proposals in ways that are understandable and acceptable to the other party, or which are at least ideologically linked.

3. **Laws, policies and political authorities** of more than one nation are involved. Often, these can be very different from those we are used to, or even directly opposed to them. Any agreements must include measures to address these differences; arbitration clauses, specification of the governing laws, taxes, etc.

4. **Participation or intervention of governmental authorities** are unique to each country. A market economy or capitalist society has more freedom than state-controlled ones. One government's goals may be very different from another's, and interventions are created to attain these. The presence of often extensive government bureaucracies can make international negotiation processes very rigid.

5. **International ventures** are vulnerable to sudden and drastic changes. War, revolution, changes in government, currency devaluation or natural disasters can void any agreement without warning.

6. **Social insights and political awareness** are important factors in big projects. Any changes to the domestic scene of your target country could have horrendous repercussions.

7. **Different currencies** create two problems.
   a) The actual value of the prices or payments set by contract can fluctuate; causing unexpected losses or gains.
   b) Each government exercises control over the flow of domestic and foreign currencies in/out of its country, and unexpected changes to government policy can have an enormous impact on the viability of a contract.

8. **Perceptions**. Whether it is right or wrong, the moment we walk in through the door we are being stereotyped to a much greater extent than we are as nationals. Know how people from other cultures perceive your culture and nation, and recognise your perceptions of them.

9. **Time**. International negotiations take a long, long time in comparison to those at home. People can often make concessions to the other side, to hurry things along, but our counterparts may be *very patient*!

10. **Teams,** much more than loners, are viewed as a serious intent to negotiate. A lone westerner can give the impression that the negotiations are not being taken seriously, and/or is not very prepared.

Principal cultural negotiating differences

- Some cultures prefer to start with agreement on general principles.

- Others prefer to address each issue individually.

- Some cultures prefer to negotiate by 'building up' from a minimum proposal.

- Others prefer to 'drill down' from a more comprehensive opening proposal.

- Cultural differences show up in the preferred pacing of the negotiations and in decision-making styles.

Cultural overview

1. The **Japanese** view the purpose of negotiations as the creation of a relationship between two parties; the contract is a written reflection of that.

2. The **Americans** aim to create binding, specific rights and obligations; the written contract details these.

3. The **African** view is satisfaction, not of the end result, but of the participation; the contract is no more than the start of a relationship with no promises attached.

4. The **Latins** view negotiations as a chance to win something; the written contract outlines everybody's obligations in an ideal world (but the world isn't ideal!).

5. The **Middle East** sees the contract as the *first* step in the negotiation process.

6. The **Russians** won't renegotiate once a contract is signed.

International negotiation tips

1. Aim to build trust and take time building a relationship.

2. Remember, the more you push the longer things will take in many countries.

3. English language directness can appear very hostile to some cultures.

4. Win-win is an unknown concept for many cultures.

5. 'Horse-trading' is about finding the optimal compromise to a shared goal. Allow lots of space to manoeuvre and horse-trade.

6. Some cultures believe a compromise is morally incorrect.

7. Be an active listener – use your ears and eyes!

8. Be prepared to 'shame' your counterpart and be shamed over any inconsistencies.

9. Use emotional appeal to pride and trust, not just logic and reasoning.

10. Treat the negotiation as a process not an event.

Equality in the negotiation process

Anglo/North Western European societies select teams on the basis of equality and competence. It is acceptable for any member to speak, raise points of issue, and ask questions in the meeting. For other cultures, it is seen as impertinent, or even an insult, for a 'junior' to speak. Be aware of the status of your counterparts and how you are expected to treat them. Treat everyone with great respect, as the key decision-maker is not necessarily the lead negotiator.

Young, inexperienced men may often be in key negotiating positions. They may have strong ties, or family connections, to the other party and are trusted for the role to extract the best deal. So, don't dismiss them!

Women and negotiations

Negotiating effectiveness does not depend on a woman's individual negotiating style or skills. Rather, it is based on how she fits the foreign culture's expectations of how she should behave in negotiations.

In some cultures a woman is expected to acquiesce rather than be assertive, and this will determine how an assertive woman is initially received in any negotiation. However, research shows that if the negotiation is run effectively, these initial traditional expectations can be set aside. Success depends on how well the woman understands those expectations and modifies her style to fit in. She may need to appear a little subservient at first.

As most cultures are relationship-oriented, women stand a good chance of being successful because of their natural tendency to develop relationships, especially if they avoid being too assertive or combative. What can help women in international negotiations is to adopt such positive attributes as active listening, empathy, distinguishing between needs and positions, co-operative language, not showing anger or frustration, and reframing issues to find common ground.

CONTRACTS

'Written contract, keiyaka, are not as common in Japan as they are in the West, and even those contracts in Japan that are concluded in writing are not expected to be any more binding because of it...To the Japanese a relationship is what holds agreements together.'

(William Bohnaker, *The Hollow Doll*)

The greatest misunderstanding in international business is the word 'contract'. Too many westerners enter into foreign deals with a naïve belief that if everything is written on paper and signed, all will be well. Westerners believe that negotiations end when agreement is reached and confirmed in a document that all parties sign.

The 'western' approach

- ◆ Written legal contract.

- ◆ Precise statement.

- ◆ Stipulates responsibilities and actions of all parties.

- ◆ Specifies deadlines to be adhered to.

- ◆ Non-negotiable.

- ◆ Implementation of contract to be followed through exactly as stated.

- ◆ Disputes are subject to legal interpretation of contractual arrangements.

- ◆ Contracts are made with organisations as a whole, not with individuals.

The thinking of other cultures

♦ The handshake speaks louder than any written document.

♦ My word is my bond: a formal contract implies a mutual lack of honour/trust.

♦ This signifies an intent to do business, no more than that.

♦ The relationship can now start.

♦ Now we have a contract we can start negotiating for better terms.

♦ If circumstances change, and my obligations cannot be met; it is all right if my end of the deal changes.

♦ Disputes are subject to an emotional appeal to pride and honour.

♦ The man who signed the original agreement has left the organisation so the contract must be renegotiated.

MANAGING ACROSS CULTURES

'For a Spaniard, success lies in titles as much as in the salary, and much more than in the work'.

(Helen Wattley Ames, *Spain is Different*)

Management competence is more elusive than technical skill. It is embedded in a way of thinking which is not easily transferable across cultures. Western management practices cause endless problems and disquiet when they are imposed in many parts of the world. As **Max Messenger** points out in his book *Staffing Europe*, Danish punctuality would cause hypertension in Greece. Even within Europe there is friction at board meetings with mergers and acquisitions. Cross-cultural tensions can surface after the deal has been struck and these may not be as well understood as the economic, financial and legal issues.

As one of Deborah's Asian students on an MBA in London said: When managers from large corporates come over to my country and talk about collaboration – what they really mean is 'Do it our way'. They come to Asia saying they want to learn, but cling to their old ways of doing things, showing little ability to change their ways.

Problems arise out of the way we think about the function of management. Abstract thinking about cause and effect, coordinating activities, anticipating contingencies, and fitting new projects into an overall institutional system is clearly required in the West. Not so elsewhere. Cultural differences regarding management include:

What is the function of an organisation?

◆ A profit-making machine – everybody knows the target and goes for it like a guided missile.

◆ A social vehicle for the common good, where harmony and paternalism is the most important concept in running them.

◆ An administrating bureaucracy where everyone knows their place and doesn't step out of line.

◆ A dynamic vehicle using the innovative and creative input of its employees towards reaching a common goal.

The role of the boss

◆ The boss is always the boss. He is paid to make decisions. Whether he is right or wrong, the decision has to be his (e.g. Latin-America, Russia, India, France).

◆ The bosses are older members of the group and deserve great respect. They gather information from their subordinates and from all around them, deliberate, and then make a decision (Far East, Arab).

◆ The boss is the first amongst equals. He is the most competent for the job and proposes ideas which he expects his colleagues to challenge and analyse – participative management style (Nordic countries, Dutch, Canadians, Australians).

◆ The leader is the one who can not only do the job (probably better than anyone else), but also has the both the skills and responsibility to bring out the best in the individuals working for him. Usually a charismatic personality, people will follow where he leads (USA, UK).

Attitude towards people

Consider this:

◆ What makes you competitive or not?

◆ What gives you the edge over the competition?

◆ What keeps customers satisfied?

◆ What creates new services and working practices?

◆ What gives you a creative thrust and a competitive advantage?

◆ What wins or loses a sale?

◆ What makes you thrive, survive or nose-dive?

◆ Not what…**who**!

It's **people** who make the difference.

If you believe in that last statement, you belong to the minority group of people who treat employees as innovative, creative individuals who can contribute directly to the goals of your organisation. You probably believe good training and empowerment help them to make better choices than you, because they work at the 'coalface'.

For other cultures, empowerment cannot exist; not because people are less talented, but because their ideology doesn't permit them to use their own initiative. The boss is there to make decisions.

Individuals and teams

◆ Employee-of-the-month schemes and singling individual workers out for distinction is a recognised way of motivating the work force; bonus schemes and material rewards are used in efforts to make an individual feel valued.

◆ Singling individuals out for praise is unacceptable to cultures where collective participation is the norm. (Everyone losses face.) This can be highly distressing. Everyone takes the praise or the blame.

◆ A Japanese will often ask for help whether he needs it or not, as this is seen as a way to build trust, relationships and create *Wa* (harmony).

Reward systems

- American society and most Northern European societies have an all-pervading emphasis on achievement and the rewards that go with it. You are paid and recognised for your competence.

- Rewards are based on loyalty, how close you can become to the 'head' of the group – affiliations – personal security, financial well-being and prestige closely linked to group membership.

- Age and seniority count the most.

Knowledge transfer and learning

Different cultures value different types of knowledge and different ways of processing it. This impacts on the way people value each other and the way they learn from each other. Whilst all cultures depend on both intuitive knowledge and objective knowledge, some cultures favour one or the other. There is a cultural barrier to the transfer of knowledge, only part of which was experienced by the Nokia engineer in Asia (see Chapter 8).

Attitudes in American/Anglo/Nordic societies

- Now in the 'knowledge era'.

- High knowledge shared objectively on need to know/functional basis.

- Individual experts.

- Knowledge is power.

- Copyright, patents, and intellectual property rights belong to individual/firm.

- Knowledge can walk out the door in the heads of employees.

- Dependency on knowledge management systems.

The Far East

- Work and share knowledge in pursuit of *Wa* (harmony creation).

- You are part of a collective entity.

- Build up the total knowledge base of group through trust at *Wa* level.

- Consensus building based upon relationships and trust.

- Knowledge is not kept in the individual.

- Knowledge is for the common good – you can't steal it from an individual, hence

- there is no concept of copyright, patents, and intellectual property rights.

- Knowledge built through group discussion and group trust.

Arab, African, and Latin countries, Latin-America, France, India

- Mutual debt societies (you help me, and I owe you).

- I will give you information if you do something for me.

- Knowledge is the ultimate power and gives me my status.

- Knowledge is not to be shared lightly.

- You have to be part of my network.

- Elitist.

- Often feel 'western' attitude is an intellectual rape.

- Will cooperate with a 'western' boss – but only just!

Project management

This can be an area of great tension. Different cultures, different values, different norms, all coming together (and not behaving as expected) can create havoc and bad feeling. A few years back, the Germans and Americans were working jointly on the space programme. The Germans became increasingly frustrated at the number of meetings called by the Americans. As the Germans said, 'We were there at the first meetings, we know what we need to achieve, we've planned carefully for all contingencies, we're perfectionists, and do a good job efficiently and on time. Now please leave us alone to get on with it!' However, (to the Germans) the American attitude to the project was like 'have-a-go-heroes'; they just got cracking believing they could learn from their mistakes along the way. So, the purpose of the meetings was to keep on track, to share lessons learned, and for constant recalibration.

SELLING ON THE INTERNATIONAL STAGE

'The hierarchical nature of Indian society demands that there is a boss and that the boss should be seen to be the boss. Everyone else just does as they are told, and even if they know the boss is 100% wrong, no one will argue.'

(Gitanjali Kolanad, *Culture Shock: India*)

Do you remember how we used to feel about the double-glazing salesman? Rude, ill-educated, limited conversation with few social skills...Unfortunately, a sad fact is that when we are trying to sell abroad that is the image we project. In Britain, we might like to get down to business and focus on the outcome, but 90% of the world does not do business in this manner.

If you don't know how to manage relationships, you'll fail in most environments outside the English-speaking countries and Northern Europe. Relationships are the key: in some countries it is relationships with local officials and government; in others it is sensitivity to the importance of the family which counts.

The greatest complaint against American salesmen is that they seem very one-dimensional; focused only on the sale, and lacking worldly sophistication and finesse. They appear just like the cowboys in the movies who barge in shooting from the hip. As an Asian student of Deborah's remarked about one encounter with an American: 'All I wanted to say to this guy was "Listen to me. Listen instead of selling!"'

There are countless stories of Americans flying down to South America in the morning, trying to fix a deal and then flying back the same day. This approach to business just won't work! One Norwegian firm we know secured a huge deal over there, although their price was more expensive than the Americans. And the reason why? The Norwegians had planned to stay for a whole week and during their first meeting they did not talk about business. Our Norwegian colleagues had done their homework – they understood the need to develop a relationship built on trust and respect. They were viewed as taking the deal more seriously and respectfully than their American competitors.

However, a Finnish gentleman of our acquaintance thought his Thai hosts were not at all interested in doing business with his firm. Whenever he tried to talk business they would turn the subject to his family and his dead relatives. Unfortunately, they thought the Finn showed them little respect as he asked no questions about their family!

An English friend told us how he lost out in a sale to a Swedish firm. The salesman of the competing British firm had taken along sandwiches in his briefcase so that when it came to lunchtime he could participate in the Swedish lunch ritual of eating sandwiches at the desk. Clearly the Swedish purchasing manager felt he shared something in common with the salesman, which created a bond between them.

The key to successful selling abroad is creating a bond at the outset. We need to be far more concerned with relationship selling than we are in our own country. However, relationships is just one area of difference. It's not only how we sell but what we sell. The Americans and Anglos sell the benefit of a product. The Nordics and Germans sell the substance and quality of the product and are aghast when we don't want to buy: Why wouldn't we want to buy such a quality product? The following story highlights the differences in approach.

Deborah had an interesting experience in Austria when browsing over some jewellery. The shop owner instantly pounced on her and gave her a running commentary about each piece she seemed to be interested in: the clarity of the gem, the grade of the gold, the weight and substance, etc. In desperation she asked the man to stop. 'I need to see the pieces. I don't care what they are made of,' she cried. For her, the importance was to visualise the jewellery which she clearly couldn't do when her thought pattern was being interrupted with all those facts!

The process for Deborah was that she needed to decide for herself which pieces interested her, and then have her interest reinforced by details of quality and the skill of the craftsman, eventually arriving at a decision which to buy. This is a very British/American buying process – we buy on emotion and justify with fact, and our sales training techniques are based on this. Incidentally, Deborah left the shop without purchasing anything, as she wasn't given the space to form any emotional bond with the items – her buying process was interrupted.

In British corporate business the buying process is simplistic. If I have a good product and want to sell it to your firm, all I need do is convince the procurement manager that it's the best thing since sliced bread, and he'll take the responsibility to buy it or not. In the Far East the buying process is very complex. Patience, tolerance and sensitivity to others are absolute essentials. In China there is a system called *guanxi*. *Guanxi* is a trusted circle of people you know and with whom you have a relationship. No one does business outside of their *guanxi*. As a foreigner you need to develop a relationship with someone to have access to that circle of people; it takes a long time. However, this is real networking.

In Japan there is the famous *Ringey sho* process. The relationship you build up with your circle is based on trust at the *Wa* level; this is called *Nemawashi*. It is a process of informal consensus building based upon relationship and trust. When selling in Japan, because of *Nemawashi* and *Wa*, the buyer needs to share the information with his colleague, who shares it with his colleague, and so on until the whole process has been completed. The approval process is called *Ringey*. *Ringey sho* is a formal stamp of approval that goes on everything.

American-style pyramid selling is almost a criminal offence in South Korea and some American executives have even been jailed! The Korean family-based culture is very vulnerable to this sales technique and prosecutors successfully argued that family members could not refuse to become involved and this sales approach imposed huge obligations that they would have to honour. However, pyramid selling works well in Italy where they have a family-based culture but less face to lose.

OPERATING IN A POLITICALLY INCORRECT WORLD

'We shall not cease from exploration,
And the end of all our exploring
Will be to arrive where we started
And know the place for the first time.'

(T. S. Elliot, *Four Quartets*)

At a conference in Europe during 2003, a panel was discussing the impact of EU legislation on the new countries that had applied to join. One of the panellists was an employment agent from Hungary. He described his company's approach to recruitment in terms that caused his fellow panellists to suck in their breath. He spoke of his practice of describing, in precise detail the ideal candidate, specifying gender, age limits and even racial preferences.

When the others drew his attention to the racist/ageist/sexist nature of his approach, and how they violated the standards now current in the EU, he shrugged and said, 'That's how we work.'

It is a fact that political correctness has not yet penetrated all countries. Many practices will not be acceptable to you, but you need to come to terms with the fact that you cannot change the world overnight. Change what you can, accept what you can't, and be a beacon of hope to others.

HOW THINGS GET DONE: BRIBERY AND CORRUPTION
Corruption and bribery: Ask yourself these questions:

♦ What is it?
♦ Can you find reasons to justify it?
♦ Where do you think the money/gifts go?
♦ Why could people from a 'corrupt' society be suspicious of you?

Deborah and her husband visited Russia and were waved through the customs gate, even though most others were being stopped to have their customs declaration stamped.

When they came to leave Russia at the end of their stay, a customs official looked at their customs declaration (unstamped) and said he would have to confiscate their foreign currency and jewellery. When they protested that they had been waved through on arrival, and that the cash and jewellery had been brought into Russia from England, he just shrugged and kept repeating, 'It's your problem'. This went on for several minutes, with mounting frustration on both sides.

Finally, the Russian official decided to take direct action to resolve the situation. He asked for their dollars, removed $80 and handed the rest back. Only then did Deborah and her husband realise that, when the official said, 'It's your problem' he was expecting to be asked, 'What do we have to do to solve it?' His choice of language provided the prompt, but it could only work with people who knew the system.

Something similar happened to Phillip in Malawi. Driving a rented car out of Lilongwe, he was waved down by a policeman on the highway. The man in uniform walked around the car, checking the road tax disc and the tyres. 'Your tyre is worn,' he said finally. 'It's smooth.' Phillip got out of the car and verified that the tyre did, in fact, look illegal. The policeman's next words were interesting. He said, 'I should fine you.'

Phillip realised that the expected response would have been 'But you won't, will you?' as he handed over his driving licence, having first inserted a bribe into its folds. Instead, he asked for a receipt so that he could reclaim the fine from the car rental company. In conversation, the policeman then made it clear that they would stop any car driven by a foreigner and look for any excuse to issue a fine, as a means of raising funds for the police, or attracting a bribe (for the individual policeman).

Both the Malawian policeman and the Russian customs official were using their positions to add to their personal funds. In other poor countries, officials of all kinds charge 'fees' for doing their jobs, often with the knowledge and connivance of their employers or their government departments. By the standards of some in the West, this would amount to corruption. However, one oriental explained it like this: 'Those countries cannot afford to pay their officials well enough, so they allow them to charge end-users of their services. It is done unofficially, and in addition to any official fee that may be involved. How is that different from tipping waiters in a restaurant? Owners of restaurants get away with paying their staff low wages, knowing that they will get tips.'

Clearly, what is considered corruption in one context is perfectly acceptable in another. It is therefore wise to withhold judgement, recognise that business practices vary around the world, and take a pragmatic approach.

13

The Ten Best Tips for Doing Business Around the World

'I am often tired of myself and have a notion that by travel I can add to my personality and so change myself a little. I do not bring back from a journey quite the same self that I took.'
(Somerset Maugham,
The Gentleman in the Parlour)

Note: public holidays are approximate dates and should be treated only as a guide.

AFRICA

A huge continent with a great cultural mix; generalisations would be too sweeping to be of any value. However, be aware that a colonial past has influenced many countries in the manner of conducting business and decisions making, and forming their attitudes. The main colonists were the British, Dutch, French and Portuguese. Resurgent African traditions, old world ways, and newly found independence are creating new and exciting business cultures. The overriding criterion for successful business transactions is a well-founded relationship. Commissions, tipping and 'oiling the wheels' are common practices in most parts.

Egypt

1. Payment is expected for everything; even when someone wishes you a 'Good day'.
2. Remember any favours that you have received, and always be ready to repay in kind or deed.
3. They are a very loving and caring people; but they expect something for that.
4. There is never a direct route for anything in Egypt; everything will go through lots of pairs of hands. Bureaucracy and networks gone mad!
5. Language is very indirect; be wary of the real meaning of their 'Yes'.
6. Showing anger and frustration won't get you anywhere.
7. Punctuality is not part of the culture.
8. Don't expect reliability or dependability.
9. Don't be taken in when someone says, 'Trust me' or 'Believe me'. Language and emotions are tools to persuade and influence people; to win the argument. (Said by an Egyptian lawyer!)
10. Don't trust anyone unless it is written down and been signed. Any document, business or official, must bear the rubber stamp of a falcon upon it to be valid.

Public holidays

February 11	*Waqf el Arafat*
February 12	*Eid Al Adha*
March 5	Islamic New Year
March/April	Easter Monday
April 25	Sinai Liberation Day
May (variable)	Prophet's Birthday
May 1	Labour Day
June 18	Evacuation Day

July 23	Revolution Day
October 6	Armed Forces Day
October 24	Suez Victory Day
November 25	Eve of *Eid Al Fitr*
November 26	*Eid Al Fitr*
December 23	Victory Day
Weekend	Thursday/Friday or Friday/Saturday
Business hours	8.00–2.00 (summer); 9.00–1.00 and then 5.00–7.00 (winter)

Kenya

1. There is a strong British influence on formality and manners, though Kenyans are humorous, casual, and seemingly carefree.
2. Contacts are all important here. Build a network of references and personal relationships through organisations like the Rotary Club, Lions Club, and Chambers of Commerce.
3. Your Kenyan colleague will want to get to know you. The first meeting will be nearly all small talk and little business. Take your cues from your counterpart.
4. Be patient. Everything happens in its own time.
5. Know people's rank and title. The boss is the boss here and decision-making is largely carried out by a few top executives.
6. Personal calls and visits are expected in carrying out negotiations.
7. Eloquent correspondence and flowery phrases are the essence of the game. Being succinct can be seen as curt. Documentation is hugely important.
8. Don't expect people to act on their own initiative; they'll be waiting for an OK from the boss.

9. Don't think everyone is always arguing; loud, open and direct communication is accepted if it is good-hearted.
10. Don't expect things to be right first time.

Public holidays

January 1	New Year's Day
March/April	Good Friday (date changes every year)
March/April	Easter Monday
May 1	Labour Day
June 1	Madaraka Day
October 10	Moi Day
October 20	Kenyatta Forces Day
December 6	*Eid Al Fitr*
December 12	*Jamhuri*/Independence Day
December 25	Christmas Day
December 26	Public Holiday
Weekend	Saturday, Sunday
Business hours	8.00–5.00

Mozambique

1. Official procedures and business practices are still very Portuguese.
2. Formality and respect for elders is important. Ensure sensitivity and respect for status (at all levels).
3. Relaxed business atmosphere, where time is a plentiful commodity.
4. Very hierarchical structures. You need to determine who is the key decision-maker.
5. Everything needs a 'stamp of approval'.
6. Decision-making process takes a very long time.

7. Translate all documents into Portuguese.
8. Don't get frustrated by all the bureaucracy – that's their way.
9. Don't try to hurry things along, you will damage your deal and the relationship.
10. Don't use first names unless invited to do so.

Public holidays

January 1	New Year's Day
February 3	Heroes' Day
February 3	Women's Day
May 1	Labour Day
June 25	Independence Day
September 7	Victory Day
September 25	Armed Forces Day
November 10	Maputo City Day (Maputo only)
December 25	Family Day
Weekend	Sunday
Business hours	8.00–4.30

Nigeria

1. Two distinctive ethnic groups mean you have to deal very differently with each culture. Christian Ibos in the south (risk takers/entrepreneurs) and Muslim Hausas in the North (formal, traditional, conservative, uncomfortable with risk-taking).
2. Middlemen are the key to successful business dealing.
3. Experience, educational credentials and age are important in establishing credibility. Take care – inspect qualifications and backgrounds of prospective partners carefully!
4. Trust is important. Rapport is valued over price,

quality or other issues.

5. Verbal agreements are preferred. Follow-up in writing, but remember that flexibility is expected dealings.

6. Small talk is considered part of the greeting process.

7. *Dash*, is the name for the 'facilitation fee', that is commonplace, although officially discouraged.

8. Don't send young people to do business; age is highly respected (and associated with wisdom). You will send out a signal that the business deal isn't important enough for the elders to join in. Males are generally preferred.

9. Don't attempt to conduct business by telephone or by mail; significant business transactions are always conducted in person, otherwise you may be signalling that the business is not very important.

10. Don't be put off by seemingly heated negotiations; open and direct communication encourages hard bargaining in this part of the world.

Public holidays

January 1	New Year's Day
February 23	*Eid Al Adha*
March/April	Good Friday/Sunday/Easter Monday (date changes every year)
May 1	Labour Day
May (variable)	Prophet's Birthday
April 24	National Day
November	Start of *Ramadan* (not a holiday) (date changes every year)
December 6	*Eid Al Fitr*
December 25	Christmas Day
December 26	Boxing Day

Weekend	Saturday afternoon, Sunday
Business hours	8.00–12.30 and then 2.00–4.30

Senegal

1. Establish personal relationships with business collea-gues. Trust and contacts are the keys to doing business here. Personal visits are warmly welcomed and the most efficient way to do business.
2. Know people's status and title.
3. Meetings are formal. Business is often conducted in either French or English. Muslims pray five times a day, so your meeting might have to be halted.
4. Communication is very indirect; don't be confronta-tional. Don't ask questions that require a 'Yes' or 'No' answer. They will tell you what they think you want to hear.
5. Be patient. Time has no price tag over here. However, punctuality is respected by people who are used to doing business internationally.
6. Business cards are both presented and received with the right hand. Avoid the use of your left hand.
7. Women do hold important positions in organisations, so a foreign women doing business is acceptable.
8. Don't expect things to be right first time.
9. Don't display irritation, anger or aggression. Main-tain your composure at all times.
10. Don't put anyone in a position where they lose may face. Politeness is essential in greetings. Physical contact is important.

Public holidays

January 1	New Year's Day
April 4	Independence Day (parades and canoe races)

February 23	*Tabaski* (*Eid Al Adha*)
March 15	*Tamxarit* (Islamic New Year)
March/April	Easter Sunday/Easter Monday (date changes every year)
May 1	Labour Day (parades)
Ascension Day	Sixth Thursday after Easter
Pentecost or Whit Sunday	Seventh Sunday after Easter
Pentecost or Whit Monday	Seventh Monday after Easter
May (variable)	Prophet's Birthday
August 15	Assumption Day
November 1	All Souls' Day
November	Start of Ramadan (not a holiday)
December 6	*Korité* (*Eid Al Fitr*)
December 25	Christmas Day

Other observances:

February 11	Carnival in Dakar
December 4	Carnival in St Louis (floats, paper and wooden lanterns)

Weekend	Sunday
Business hours	9.00–1.00 and then 4.00–7.00

South Africa

1. Be prepared for bureaucratic delays and red tape.
2. Social status and qualifications are admired, but at work merit matters more than who you know.
3. Use both English and Afrikaans for promotional materials. Use English for transactions.
4. The importance, size, and stage of your business dealings dictate what level of seniority attends the meetings.

5. Present the benefits of any deal for both sides before you start the negotiations.
6. Take the time to make friends with your counterparts. Socialising before and after meetings is an important part of the business mix.
7. Mixed race/gender teams are good for negotiating. White and black South Africans behave very differently.
8. Don't use lawyers at your meetings; people do business based on trust established during negotiations to ensure that all details agreed upon are adhered to. (Generally, contracts aren't very detailed.)
9. Don't be surprised or fooled by the 'take it or leave it' attitude; this is their bargaining tactic.
10. Don't pressurise with deadlines; this may result in more delays than you anticipated!

Public holidays:

January 1	New Year's Day
March 21	Human Rights Day
March/April	Good Friday (date changes every year)
March/April	Easter
April 1	Family Day
April 27	Freedom Day
May 1	Workers' Day
June 16	Youth Day
August 9	National Women's Day
September 24	Heritage Day
December 16	Day of Reconciliation
December 25	Christmas Day
December 26	Goodwill Day

Weekend	Saturday, Sunday
Business hours	8.00–5.00 (1 hour for lunch)

Zimbabwe

1. Negotiations take a long time; decision-making is by consensus.
2. Meetings are for the satisfaction of taking part and saying your piece.
3. Take time to build relationships on all levels; you never know who influences the final outcome of a deal.
4. Socialising is an important part of doing business; people like to be seen as good hosts.
5. Know everyone's status.
6. Power is the name of the game.
7. Don't try and do things your way; they'll make you do it theirs and you will have wasted time.
8. Don't get frustrated with the bureaucracy.
9. Don't get short tempered with any government officials; they might try to block you, as they wield the power.
10. Don't pass by strangers without a nod or a greeting. It's considered bad manners.

Public holidays

January 1	New Year's Day
March/April	Good Friday to Easter Monday (date changes every year)
April 18	Independence Day
May 1	Workers' Day
May 25	Africa Day
August 11	Heroes' Day
August 12	Armed Forces Day
December 22	Unity Day

December 25	Christmas Day
December 26	Boxing Day
Weekend	Saturday, Sunday
Business hours	8.00–4.30

ASIA

In this part of the world the countries have a common colonial heritage and many of the prevailing attitudes derive from that heritage. The richer, more educated people are very elitist and the poorer classes are very conscious of knowing their place in the multilayered social structure. They accept bribery as a part of normal exchange and view it as commission, not corruption. All these attitudes impact greatly the way business is carried out, with whom, and how things get done.

India

1. Business is conducted at a snail's pace. Be prepared for a good deal of discussion, followed by a long wait for a final decision.
2. A handshake signals an agreement; but business contracts will be scrutinised and this can take weeks or months.
3. A direct 'No' is never possible; Indians will say many things that sound like 'Yes' but aren't!
4. Phrase questions carefully, i.e. 'Where does this road lead?' not 'Does this road go to Mombai?' Indian responses can be ambiguous; they'll tell you what they think you want to hear so as not to upset you.

5. Always budget for 'commissions'; you will be expected to pay for any introductions or favours. These payments grease the wheel.

6. Indians are often seen as the best negotiators; they'll drive a hard bargain, and then drive it some more! Negotiating teams are led by management and supported by technical experts. High-level management make the decisions but they may not be represented on the team. Middle managers do make some input into the decision. Incentives will help the process.

7. Relationships are important, along with good contacts for business. Building trust is vital.

8. A win/win approach is aimed at, though compromise is acceptable, but trust makes everyone flexible.

9. Don't expect people to use their initiative and make things happen; strong fatalism and predestiny play a large part in people's thinking.

10. Don't give criticism as Indians easily take offence; be sensitive to, and respectful of, the concept of face. Harmony is extremely important.

Public holidays

January 1	New Year's Day
January 14	*Makara Sakrankti*
January 14	*Pongal*
January 26	Republic Day
February 17	*Vasant Panchami/Sri Panchami*
February 23	*Eid ul Zuha* or *Adha*
March 13	*Maha Shivaratri*
March 24	*Muharram* or *Ashoora*
March 28	*Holi*

March/April	Good Friday (date changes every year)
April 14	*Baisakhi, Vishu/Bahag, Mesadi, Maghi*
April 21	*Sri Rama Navami*
April 25	*Mahavir Jayanthi*
May (variable)	*Milad un Nabi* or *Eid ul Milad* (The Prophet's Birthday)
August 15	Independence Day
August 22	*Raksha Bandhan*
August 31	*Krishna Janamashti* or *Janmastami*
September 10	*Ganesh Chaturthi/Vinayaka Chaturthi*
October 2	Mahatma Gandhi's Birthday
October 15	*Dussehra (Vijaya Dashmi)*
November 4	*Diwali (Deepavali)*
November 6	*Bhai Duj*
November 19	Guru Nanak's Birthday
December 6	*Eid ul Fitr*
December 25	Christmas Day
Weekend	Saturday, Sunday
Business hours	9.30–5.00

Pakistan
1. Focused negotiations and hard bargaining.
2. Pakistan is a large bureaucracy and business is conducted at a slow pace.
3. Build personal relationships before attempting to accomplish your business deals. Trust is all important.
4. Expect to pay, and budget for, services rendered, introductions made, etc. The euphemistic and ethical justification for paying these 'bribes' is treating them like sales commission.

5. Expect a few meetings to take place before you can secure a deal.
6. Contracts should be drawn up in both English and the local language of the region e.g. Urdu or Punjabi.
7. Don't worry if the other person challenges your every claim and checks and verifies everything in detail before coming to a decision.
8. Don't turn down tea offered at a meeting; it's considered very impolite.
9. Don't joke during meetings; it's considered rude.
10. Don't ask direct personal questions, especially about the women in their family.

Public holidays

February 23	*Eid Al Adha*
March 15	Islamic New Year
March 23	Pakistan Day
March 24	*Ashoora*
March/April	Good Friday/Easter/Easter Monday (date changes every year)
May 1	Labour Day
May (variable)	Prophet's Birthday
August 14	Independence Day
September 6	Defence of Pakistan Day
September 11	Anniversary of the Death of Qaid-i-Azam
November	Start of *Ramadan* (not a holiday) date changes every year
November 9	Birthday of Allama Iqbal (National Poet)
December 6	*Eid Al Fitr*
December 25	Birthday of Qaid i-Azam (general holiday)

	Christmas Day (Christians only)
December 26	Boxing Day (Christians only)
Weekend	Friday
Business hours	9.00–4.00 (summer 7.30–2.30)

Sri Lanka

1. Rapport and trust are necessary to move business along; this takes time to establish.
2. Socialising comes before any negotiations.
3. Both Sinhalese (Buddhists) and Tamils (Hindus) use traditional and religious beliefs, in combination with their personal feelings and current circumstances, to determine the truth and make decisions. Rules and facts are not absolute.
4. People tend to place importance on the group and on an individual's position and rank within the group.
5. Responsibility to the self and to personal relationships is high up on the agenda when the Sinhalese make important business decisions.
6. For the Tamils, an individual's responsibility to the group (the family, social group and religion) is of paramount concern.
7. Business women are rare here but you will be treated with respect.
8. Don't try to hurry things; business moves slowly, delays are frequent, and many trips are necessary.
9. Don't be surprised if your counterpart consults an astrologer before making any important decisions.
10. Don't refuse any refreshment offered at the beginning of your meeting; this is a sign of goodwill. Compliment your host as a sign of your appreciation.

Public holidays

January 14	*Tamil Thai Pongal*
February 4	National Day or Independence Day
February 23	*Eid al Adha*
March/April	Good Friday (date changes every year)
April 13	Sinhala/Tamil New Year's Eve
April 14	Sinhala/Tamil New Year
May 1	May Day
May (variable)	*Milad un Nabi* or *Eid ul Milad* – The Prophet's Birthday
May 26-27	*Vesak* (and the following day)
December 6	*Eid al Fitr*
December 25	Christmas Day
Weekend	Saturday, Sunday
Business hours	8.30–4.30/5.00

AUSTRALIA/NEW ZEALAND

These two countries follow western business practices, place heavy emphasis on individuality and adhere to the 'norms' of British business. Few people speak any language other than English. A very distinct accent and slang has developed 'down under' which can be difficult for non-native speakers of English, used to American TV, to understand. Best times to visit on business are February to May or October to November.

Australia

1. Business is conducted quickly. Any small talk (usually sport or current affairs) is usually brief and negotiating is a brief process.
2. The country is so large that contacts and connections

are very useful. There is an Australian version of the 'Old Boy' network among senior industrial executives.

3. Australians are hard working and strive for a better quality of life. Leisure time is important to them, as is sport and recreational activities.

4. Time is precious, not to be wasted. Be punctual.

5. Once a contract is drawn up both parties are expected to adhere to it. Australian commercial law is very thorough and detailed.

6. Be aware: Australians are poor on foreign languages.

7. Everyone is equal and status can be treated with irreverence. Australians do not practise deference! Informality is the etiquette.

8. Australians are pragmatic. If you have a problem, don't conceal it. Presentations should be complete – the good and the bad.

9. Don't be off put by the directness in communication. Australians are blunt to the point of being rude. This is not meant to offend. Respond with confidence and good humour.

10. Don't lose your nerve when bargaining. Price haggling is common and everyone is looking for the best deal.

Public holidays

January 1	New Year's Day*
January 26	Australia Day*
March/April	Good Friday (date changes every year)
March/April	Easter Saturday**
March/April	Easter Sunday
March/April	Easter Monday
April 25	ANZAC Day*

June	Second Monday Queen's birthday (except Western Australia)
December 25	Christmas Day*
December 26	Boxing Day (except Southern Australia)

*If these holidays fall on a Saturday or Sunday, they are observed on the Monday following.
**Except Western Australia and Victoria.

| Weekend | Saturday afternoon, Sunday |
| Business hours | 9.00–5.00 |

State holidays
Australian Capital Territory (Canberra)

March	Third Monday Canberra Day
August	First Monday Bank Holiday
October	First Monday Labour Day

New South Wales

| August | First Monday Bank Holiday |
| October | First Monday Labour Day |

Northern Territory

May	First Monday May Day
July	First Friday Alice Springs Show (Alice Springs only)
July	Second Friday Tennant Creek Show (Tennant Creek only)
July	Third Friday Katherine Show (Katherine only)
July	Fourth Friday Darwin Show (Darwin only)
August	First Monday Picnic Day

Queensland

May	First Monday Labour Day

Brisbane

The Royal National (RNA) Show takes place 2nd week of August and is a holiday there.

South Australia

May 18	Adelaide Cup Day (Adelaide only)
October	First Monday Labour Day
December 26	Proclamation Day

Tasmania

February	Secodnd Tuesday Regatta Day (South only)
February	Last Wednesday Launceston Cup Day (North only)
March	First Monday Eight Hours Day
April 14	Bank Holiday
October	Thursday after 17th Hobart Show Day (South only)
November 2	Recreation Day (North only)

Launceston

The Launceston show takes place in early October and is a holiday there.

Victoria

March	Second Monday Labour Day
November 1st	Tuesday Melbourne Cup Day (Melbourne metro area only)

Western Australia

March	First Monday Labour Day
June	First Monday Foundation Day

September   Monday nearest 30th Queen's
                   birthday

Celebrations
May   Second Sunday Mother's Day
September   First Sunday Father's Day

New Zealand

1. A friendly and honest people, who are polite, formal and reserved. Be decorous and respectful of 'appropriate' behaviour. Business dress is conservative.
2. Cultural mix of British reserve, Maori graciousness, and US-style openness. Rank is minimised, equality emphasised, and individual achievement and initiative are encouraged.
3. Punctuality is important. Arrive 5 minutes early – that is the custom.
4. Business pace is fast compared with Australia.
5. Negotiations are conducted in an honest, frank, and forthright manner. Present clearly and pay attention to details.
6. Contracts are legally binding and both parties are expected to adhere to the agreement.
7. Introductory meetings take place in an office, after that in a restaurant over lunch.
8. Little attention is paid to wealth and status. You are judged by the person you are. Your word must be your bond.
9. Don't use first names initially. Once a relationship has been established, you can start using first names quickly.
10. Don't confuse or compare New Zealanders with Australians. Different country, different people,

different culture! Strong rivalry exists between the two.

Public holidays

January 1	New Year's Day
January 2	Second Day of New Year
February 6	Waitangi Day
March/April	Good Friday/Easter Sunday/Easter Monday
April 25	ANZAC Day
June 2	Queen's birthday
October	Last Monday Labour Day
December 25	Christmas Day
December 26	Boxing Day
Weekend	Saturday afternoon, Sunday
Business hours	8.30/9.00–5.00/5.30 (Saturdays 9.00–12.30)

CENTRAL AMERICA

'Machismo' and the public face of a man are of overriding importance in this part of the world. Honour and pride, trust and relationships, are the driving factors in business. Status is the motivator. Time is fluid. Women are not regarded as equals and men make decisions for them.

Guatemala

1. Quiet and respectful behaviour is expected; ask questions quietly, be patient and never raise your voice, or insult anyone. Remember face and harmony are valued here.
2. Translate your brochures and promotional literature into Spanish.

3. Take time to establish a personal relationship with your business counterpart; this is a must.

4. Mutual contacts can help business flow, especially during initial introductions. They add credibility to your dealings.

5. The 'talking stone' is a part of Guatemalan culture. You need to pick this up before you can say something in a meeting.

6. The corruption index is quite high so be prepared to 'oil the wheels' and pay for favours.

7. Although a 'macho' society, business women will be treated with respect as long as you demonstrate decorous behaviour. Men usually represent women in all matters here.

8. Don't be confrontational or show anger or displeasure, however frustrated you may become.

9. Don't discuss business around family events; leave it for the office or over a meal.

10. Don't make comparisons between Guatemala and other parts of Central America. Get to know it for itself; this demonstrates respect and sensitivity.

Public holidays

January 1	New Year's Day
March/April	Easter Sunday (date changes every year)
May 1	Labour Day
June 30	Army Day
August 15	Assumption of the Blessed Virgin Mary (in Guatemala City only)
September 15	Independence Day
October 20	Revolution Day

November 1	All Saints' Day
December 24	Christmas Eve (afternoon only)
December 25	Christmas Day
December 31	New Year's Eve (afternoon only)
Weekend	Saturday, Sunday
Business hours	8.00–noon and then 2.00–6.00

Celebrations
Easter Week is the fiesta of Guatemala City.
All Saints' Day is a fiesta in Todos Santos.

Honduras

1. Establish long-term relationships based on mutual trust and reliability.
2. Extensive negotiations, and many trips, may be necessary to complete your deal. The same person must be involved each time.
3. Ask open questions which require detailed answers, as 'Yes/No' answers will be ambiguous. They want to please you and will tell you what they think you want to hear.
4. Make an emotional appeal, emphasising trust, mutual compatibility, the benefits to a person's pride, etc. This will be more effective than emphasising profit and gain.
5. Very status driven, so make sure you have people of equal status conducting business. It's an insult to send a 'junior' even though they may be the best person for the job.
6. Compromise is seen as a weakness and possible loss of face.
7. Hondurans place importance on their emotional

reactions to projects and the people involved in them.

8. The decision-making process is strongly affected by the need to maintain group harmony. The collective group and a person's role within the social system is very important – not initiative or expertise.

9. Don't expect speedy progress.

10. Don't reply with a direct 'No'. The communication is indirect, always polite, and ensuring no loss of face. Say, 'Maybe' or 'We'll see'.

Public holidays

January 1	New Year's Day
March/April	Holy Thursday (date changes every year)
March/April	Good Friday/Easter Sunday
April 14	Panamerican Day
May 1	Labour Day
September 15	Independence Day
October 3	Morazon Day
October 12	Columbus Day
October 21	Army Day
December 25	Christmas Day
Weekend	Saturday, Sunday
Business hours	7.30–4.30

Nicaragua

1. Everything happens at a much slower pace than 'western' societies.

2. Your *enchufados* (contacts) are your lifeblood in everything you do.

3. Spend a lot of time making your contacts, investing in personal relationships and networking; who you know

is more important than what you know.

4. Rules and regulations depend on circumstances.

5. Nicaraguans are very suspicious of outsiders' information, logic and perspectives.

6. Decision-making is done from a subjective and personal perspective.

7. Don't rely on facts and logic; they don't have a lot of relevance.

8. Don't expect reason to make sense; make emotional appeals, call on trust, build mutual compatibility, inflame pride.

9. Don't be offended by a lack of respect for women; this is a very macho society and business women are rare. Act professionally and respect will soon be yours.

10. Don't try to appeal to an individual's well-being; the common good is the name of the game.

Public holidays

January 1	New Year's Day
March/April	Holy Thursday/Good Friday/Sunday (date changes every year)
May 1	Labour Day
May 30	Mothers' Day
July 19	National Liberation Day
August 1	Fiesta Day
September 14	San Jacinto Fight Day
September 15	Independence Day
November 1	All Souls' Day
December 8	Immaculate Conception
December 25	Christmas Day
Weekend	Saturday afternoon, Sunday
Business hours	8.00–6.00, (Saturdays 8.00–noon)

EASTERN EUROPE AND THE BALKANS

The speed of thinking and working is a lot slower than in Western Europe. Although people use email, they will check this once a week. It is difficult to get a firm commitment to a meeting; this is a power play. You will be asked to phone on the day, then again later in the morning, and again in the afternoon. A typical response is: 'I may be busy, so I can't tell you now'. Business activity grinds to a near halt during the latter part of July and most of August for extended summer holidays. You need to know how to get around the gatekeepers. Bribing is commonplace and people are suspicious of you if you do not participate. Don't get frustrated at the amount of time spent drinking coffee during the working day.

Bosnia

1. People are friendly and make eye contact in all transactions.
2. Business practices are uniformly western.
3. Business meetings should be scheduled more towards the morning hours. During the summer months, do not schedule meetings late on Fridays as workers tend to leave early. It is commonplace to transact business in a restaurant.
4. Personal relationships will influence business decisions. Business relationships are founded on trust; significant time and energy must be invested to establish this.
5. Business moves very slowly, or not at all, due to the cumbersome bureaucracy and general socio-economic collapse.
6. Some business people are quick to recognise oppor-

tunities and will act quickly to not waste time.

7. Communication is not a major problem, as English is popular as a second language.

8. Management is typically concentrated at the level of the MD – the key decision maker.

9. Don't use first names. Only good friends do this; use conventional and professional titles.

10. Don't assume a legal contract will be binding. Contract law at present may be unenforceable. Privatisation, and legal, regulatory, and judicial reform are in the process of change.

Public holidays

January 1	New Year's Day
February 12	*Eid Al Adha* (Muslims only)
March 8	International Women's Day
March/April	Easter Sunday
May 1	International Labour Day
November 26	*Eid Al Fitr* (Muslims only)
December 25	Christmas Day
Weekend	Saturday, Sunday
Business hours	8.00–6.00 (plus every first Saturday of the month)

Croatia

1. Croatia is a conservative region, with a very proud, hospitable, and warm-hearted people. Generally they are well-educated and cultured. English is widely spoken, with many young managers fluent in it.

2. Business tends towards formal protocol, though is somewhat relaxed. The boss is the boss. Hierarchies exist. There is little delegation of authority.

3. Decision-making is centralised, resting in the hands of a managing director or general manager. Don't assume a negotiation is completed until you have dealt with the top management.

4. Croatian firms tend to rely on their traditional business relationships. Price may not be the controlling factor in the decision process if experience with one supplier has been satisfactory before.

5. Organisations are a mixed image of western-style efficiency and cumbersome bureaucracy. There is a lot of behind-the-scenes power and pulling of strings.

6. Punctuality is important. Meetings usually keep to time.

7. There are a large number of local agents, advisers, and consultants willing to act for foreign companies, thoroughly check them out in advance.

8. Exchange business cards with formal introductions, and as with many European countries, print your titles, professional and academic qualifications on them.

9. Don't expect transactions to be made quickly. Although there is an element of spontaneity, a bureaucratic mentality gets in the way.

10. Don't think of Croatia as a war-torn country needing to be saved. It has a long and proud history which contributes to respected traditions and a deep sense of culture.

Public holidays

January 1	New Year's Day
January 6	Epiphany
March/April	Easter Sunday and Monday
May 1	May Day

May 30	Independence Day (Statehood Day)
June 22	Antifascist Struggle
August 5	National Thanksgiving Day
August 15	Assumption
November 1	All Saints' Day
December 25	Christmas Day
December 26	Second Day of Christmas
Weekend	Saturday, Sunday
Business hours	8.00–7.00 (1 hour for lunch)

Hungary

1. Securing a business deal can take an unpredictable length of time. Under the old communist regime, decisions would take months. Once they have agreed to a contract Hungarians will keep their word and fulfil the agreement.
2. Hungarians appreciate face-to-face business dealings, where intentions, feelings and opinions can be expressed openly.
3. They look for trust and lasting relationships, and these come before stringent adherence to rules and regulations. They are a warm and generous people.
4. Hungarians do not say 'No' outright. Interpret 'Maybe' or a change of topic as a refusal.
5. Spontaneity is valued. Agendas are flexible. Meetings start on time, more or less.
6. Hierarchy and class prevail here. People talk about the 'intelligentsia'.
7. Business deals are completed/rounded off with eating and drinking, handshakes and embraces.
8. Find a trusted local contact who can introduce you to his/her network, and work on establishing a secure

bond. Hungarians like to do business with people they know through their network.

9. Don't expect people to take responsibility; bosses still make decisions. A hangover from the communist system means many people think that they have little control over their lives and look to others to make things happen.

10. Don't refuse the brandy served during negotiations.

Public holidays

January 1	New Year's Day
March 15	National Day
March/April	Easter Sunday (date changes every year)
March/April	Easter Monday
May 1	Labour Day
May	Whit Sunday (Pentecost: seventh Sunday after Easter)
May	Whit Monday (day following Pentecost)
August 20	Constitution Day
October 23	Republic Day
November 1	All Saints' Day
December 25	Christmas Day
December 26	Boxing Day
Weekend	Saturday afternoon and Sunday
Business hours	8.30–5.00 (Saturdays 8.30–1.30)

Non-holiday observances

August 20	St Stephen of Hungary

Macedonia

1. Building strong, personal relationships is very impor-

tant and will influence success of business transactions.

2. On the surface firms practice 'western-style' management, but everything is slow and cumbersome.

3. There are a lot of entrepreneurs setting up in business and being successful at wheeling and dealing.

4. A consultative decision-making process belies the fact that the head of the company will make his own decision. Ask who is the key decision-maker.

5. Meetings are less formal than in Western Europe and are frequently combined with a meal.

6. Who you know is more important than what you know. How you dress will be noticed.

7. Punctuality is not precise. It is a great effort to get people to adhere rigidly to times and Macedonians find it incomprehensible that Nordic people think tardiness is disrespectful.

8. Women make up a substantial part of the workforce and enjoy a more egalitarian status than other parts of the region. As a foreign visitor, a woman would be better off eating in a hotel rather than alone in a restaurant.

9. Don't use first names; only family and close friends use them, and the use of titles/surnames show respect.

10. Don't be surprised if you never get what you ask for. You may describe precisely what you require, but you will be given what they think you ought to have!

Public holidays

January 1	New Year's Day
January 6	Orthodox Christmas Eve
January 7	Orthodox Christmas Day
January 14	Old New Year

February 12	*Eid Al Adha* (Muslims only)
March 8	International Women's Day
March/April	Good Friday/Easter Sunday/Easter Monday
May 1	May Day
May 24	St Cyrilus and Methodius Day
August 2	Ilinden (St Elijah's Uprising Day)
September 8	Independence Day
November 26	*Eid Al Fitr* (Muslims only)
Weekend	Saturday afternoon, Sunday
Business hours	8.00–7.00/8.00 (Saturdays 8.00–2.00)

Romania

1. Romanians are quite formal. First names are used by close friends and relatives. Address your business counterpart by their last name and title only.
2. Send letters in English, these are more respected than documents written in Romanian. Present your business card to every business person you meet. Have academic titles and your degrees printed on them.
3. Punctuality is respected, though not always observed. Schedule meetings beforehand, always try to get confirmation of an appointment in writing.
4. Examine the business credentials of the firm/person you are dealing with to ensure legitimacy. Once a relationship is established your business partner/agent will be loyal for a long time.
5. French is the favoured second language. Bring an interpreter to all negotiations unless you speak a common language.
6. After the agreement and contracts are drawn up, they will still be subject to approval by senior executives of

the organisation/firm. Negotiations and decisions are based on business facts.

7. Dress and appearance are very important. You have to look the part, but generally dress is conservative. Stay in the best hotels, Romanians are impressed by prestige.

8. Don't get frustrated at the slow pace in business dealings. Romanians are unused to western business practices; they also have a distrust of authority after years of authoritarian rule.

9. Don't get offended. Opinions are openly and freely expressed; a sign that you can be trusted with their truth.

10. Don't be surprised; the practice of *baksheen* (tipping) is common, especially when negotiating with Romanian officials.

Public holidays

January 1/2	New Year's Day
January 6	Epiphany
March/April	Easter Sunday and Monday
May 1	Labour Day
December 1	National Day
December 25	Christmas Day
December 26	Second Day of Christmas
Weekend	Saturday afternoon, Sunday
Business hours	8.00–4.00 (Saturdays 8.00–12.30)

EUROPE

The Nordic countries

The Nordic countries are very different from the rest of Europe in their attitudes and behaviour and it is useful to mention this at the outset. The Nordic region comprises Norway, Sweden, Finland, Denmark and Iceland. They are all driven by a strong work ethic, are exceptionally honest, and are very tolerant of people who are different from them. The two things they deplore are bribery/corruption (dishonest) and tardiness (disrespectful). They believe in working towards the common good and looking after those who are more unfortunate than themselves. However, they are 'straight' talkers and this can be seen as being very brusque. July is the holiday month.

The North/South divide

There is a distinct difference between the southern countries of Europe and the rest. In the south, the pace of business is much slower and unpredictable. Time is to be enjoyed. Relationships and emotions play a large part in influencing the success of business deals. Both Italy and Spain are beginning to adopt a more time-efficient/'professional' approach to business to boost their economies. The southern countries are sometimes regarded as not being completely trustworthy; this is because their values are very different from the rule-bound north. August is the holiday month.

Denmark

1. The pace of business is slow. Business is conducted efficiently; straight to the point with little small talk.
2. Punctuality is extremely important – arrive exactly on time (even at social gatherings).
3. The Danes are meticulous and love details. Presentations should address all aspects of the business proposal.

4. Respecters of traditions and heritage; promote how well-established your firm is (put founding date on your business card) and its reputation.
5. Logic and reason is used for decision-making.
6. Communication is open, direct and straightforward. Eye contact is important.
7. Danes are relatively informal, but use titles when you first meet someone.
8. Danes are seen as the 'Italians of the North' by other Nordic countries – not to be completely trusted to get things done. Proud, honest, efficient but not always effective.
9. Don't openly criticise anyone/any culture. The Danes are very tolerant of others.
10. Don't make personal comments, even compliments, as they can be seen as invasive.

Public holidays

January 1	New Year's Day
March/April	Holy Thursday (*Skær* Thursday)
March/April	Good Friday/Easter Sunday/Easter Monday
April 26	Common Prayer Day
Ascension Day	Sixth Thursday after Easter
May	Whit Sunday/Monday (Pentecost: seventh Sunday after Easter)
June 5	Constitution Day/Fathers' Day (from midday, also bank holiday)
December 24	Christmas Eve
December 25	Christmas Day
December 26	Second Day of Christmas
December 27	Third Day of Christmas

December 31	New Year's Eve
Weekend	Saturday and Sunday
Business hours	8.00/9.00–4.30/5.30

Non-holiday observances

April 16	Birthday of the Queen (not a public holiday)
May	Second Sunday Mothers' Day

Finland

1. Finns maintain high ideals of loyalty and reliability. They take promises and agreements seriously. An agreement by handshaking is a legal commitment. Try to do all negotiating with the managing director of the firm. He is the head of the firm and will make all decisions.

2. You might think you've got a win-win deal with a Finn, but in reality he will get the better end of the deal. They are known for being tough but fair.

3. They're nice people and are driven by good, ethical values and hard work. They are also incredibly honest and dependable.

4. Very little small talk during negotiations. Business is attended to almost immediately. Outward displays of emotion are inappropriate. Always remain calm.

5. In presentations expect to give a good account of your firm's background and adherence to good working practices. Don't be put off by the silence at the end and lack of questions. If it was important you would have mentioned it in your presentation!

6. Finns speak bluntly, assertively and honestly, demonstrating their respect for you; i.e. you can take

straightforward discussions. Assertiveness is respected, but aggression not. Stick up for yourself and you should find they will compromise. They are uncomfortable with direct, sustained eye contact.

7. They want action, rather than empty words. Ask for 'time to think' if things are moving a little too quickly for you.

8. Don't use 'high sounding' or impressive rhetoric. Communication is open, direct, and to the point. Use concise and explicit language.

9. Don't be put off by long silences. This is normal. Finns like to think over what has been discussed and will always take a moment to think before they speak.

10. Don't be ostentatious or boastful. This is seen as pushy, completely unseemly, and is *always* inappropriate.

Public holidays

January 1	New Year's Day
January 6	Epiphany
March/April	Good Friday/Easter Sunday/Easter Monday date changes every year
May 1	May Day or *Vappu*[1]
Ascension Day	Sixth Thursday after Easter
May	Whit Sunday (Pentecost: seventh Sunday after Easter)
June	First Friday after 18th June Midsummer's Eve or *Juhannusaatto*[2]
June	Saturday following Midsummer's Day is *Juhannuspaiva*
November	Saturday following October 30 All Saints Day

December 6	Independence Day
December 24	Christmas Eve (from midday)
December 25	Christmas Day
December 26	Second day of Christmas
Weekend	Saturday and Sunday
Business hours	8.00–4.30

[1] Vappu is really the night of 30 April to 1 May so there may not be too many people working in the afternoon of 30 April.

[2] Partial holiday only.

Celebrations

May	Second Sunday Mothers' Day
November	Second Sunday Fathers' Day

France

1. The French are very formal and reserved. They like titles and academic credentials.
2. Negotiating takes time and plenty of discussion. You will be made to feel like a supplicant (don't take it personally!), this is what gives the French their 'arrogant' reputation.
3. Hierarchies are very strict; everybody knows their place and bosses are left to make decisions. This is the birth place of bureaucracies.
4. Make your presentations very formal, logical and well-argued.
5. Thinking is a well respected activity. You will be challenged about your point of view, so argue logically with no appeal to emotion or trust to win respect.
6. Deadlines are unimportant to the French. The quality of the thought/product is more important than having

things finished on time.

7. In all things, time is flexible and fluid.
8. Don't lose your temper. The French like to keep their emotions in check, keeping calm and reserved.
9. Don't mistake animated gestures and loud voices for temper; this is showing great interest.
10. Don't try to rush the French, everything happens in its own time. Lots of general conversation and talking needs to take place first.

Public holidays

January 1	New Year's Day
March/April	Good Friday/Easter Sunday/Easter Monday
May 1	Labour Day
May 8	Victory Day of 1945, end of the Second World War in Europe
Ascension Day	Sixth Thursday after Easter
Whit Sunday	Seventh Sunday after Easter
Pentecost	Seventh Monday after Easter
July 14	French National Day (Bastille Day)
August 15	Assumption Day (of the Virgin Mary)
November 1	All Saints' Day
November 11	Armistice Day of 1918
December 25	Christmas Day
Weekend	Saturday afternoon and Sunday
Business hours	8.30/9.00–6.30/7.00 with two hours for lunch

If a holiday falls on a Tuesday or Thursday then most companies will close for a four-day weekend, called 'making the bridge' (*faire le pont*). Sometimes offices close at noon before a holiday.

Celebrations

Mother's Day	Last Sunday in May
Father's Day	Second or third week after Mother's Day
Le nouveau Beaujolais est arrivé	Third Thursday in November. The new Beaujolais wine is for sale – lots of parties in bars
November 25	St Catherine, day for single women. Funny hats
January 6	Epiphany – *Fête des Rois*. Visit of the Wise Men/Magi to the newborn Christ

Germany

1. Pay great attention to detail, order and planning.
2. Discipline and self-control gain respect, as do such traditional values as duty, obedience and loyalty.
3. The Germans are very formal. Use titles, academic credentials, and always knock on doors before entering.
4. Great hierarchies exist in organisations and the more senior a boss is, the more formal and reserved he behaves.
5. Business negotiations are technical and factual in content and delivery.
6. Decisions and conclusions are made before a meeting by experts you will not meet.
7. Be punctual for every appointment – business or social. Two or three minutes late is insulting.
8. Germans like to 'do their homework' before explain-

ing something in detail. Explanations tend to be lengthy and complex.

9. Don't try to change their minds. Decisions take a long time to make and deliberate; once made, they are unchangeable.

10. Don't use humour and little anecdotes to help things flow. This is seen to demean the importance of the business transactions. The Germans do have a sense of humour – but at 'appropriate' times and places, and nearly always in private.

Public holidays

January 1	New Year's Day
March/April	Good Friday/Easter Sunday/Easter Monday (date changes every year)
May 1	Labour Day
Ascension Day	Sixth Thursday after Easter
May	Whit Sunday Pentecost: seventh Sunday after Easter
May	Whit Monday day following Pentecost
October 3	German Unity Day
December 25	Christmas Day
December 26	Second Christmas Day
Weekend	Saturday and Sunday
Business hours	8.00/9.00–4.00/5.00

Holidays only observed in some federal states/some only observed in Catholic areas

January 6	New Year's Day
May/June	Corpus Christi (*Fronleichnam*)
August 15	Assumption
October 31	Reformation Day (only celebrated in

	Protestant areas)
November 1	All Soul's Day
November 18	Repentance Day (only celebrated by Saxony)

Celebrations

Oktoberfest	End of September and ends in October
Weinfeste	September, wine festivals that are celebrated in the wine regions
November 11	Beginning of carnival celebrations in Catholic regions. Businesses shut down in certain cities

Greece

1. The Greeks are good at bargaining; great patience and excellent bargaining skills are two vital ingredients needed when negotiating with them.
2. Posturing and bragging are part of the culture, so you will need to do the same. Don't try to be humble or modest.
3. Time is elastic and meant to be enjoyed, not spent! A good meeting will last for ever, so don't arrange lots of meetings in any one day.
4. Take lots of business cards and hand them out all the time. Shake hands when meeting and leaving, and whenever else you can fit it in. The Greeks are very tactile.
5. Age and seniority command great respect. Senior executives make all the firm's decisions, even to choosing the crockery!
6. The boss is the decision-maker. He responds to appeals of emotion and trust – not logic and

evidence. He'll buy because he likes you, not because your product is cheaper (but he'll drive a good price in the end).

7. Greek gestures for 'yes/no' are easily misinterpreted, so confirm in language your mutual understanding. Nodding and shaking the head mean the opposite in Greece.

8. Don't be offended if you are asked 'invasive' personal questions, such as how much you earn and how much something cost. (This is part of the posturing process, and your answer need not be true!)

9. Don't misinterpret a smile; this can be controlled anger.

10. Don't refuse any alcohol you are offered during your meeting. Drinking together creates a bond of friendship.

Public holidays

January 1	New Year's Day
January 6	Epiphany
March 18	Clean Monday (start of Lent)
March 25	Greek Independence Day
March/April	Good Friday (except shops which open after 2 pm) March/April
March/April	Easter Sunday/Monday
March/April	Easter Tuesday (half day for shops only)
May 1	May Day
June	Holy Ghost (Monday after Pentecost: seventh Sunday after Easter
August 15	Assumption of the Blessed Virgin Mary

September 13	Finding of the True Cross, Mytilene (Lesbos)
October 28	*Ochi* Day
December 25	Christmas Day
December 26	Second day of Christmas
Weekend	Sunday
Business hours	8.00–1.30 and then 4.00–7.00 (5.00–8.00 in summer)

Italy

1. The boss is the boss. All decisions come from the top and organisations are very hierarchical. Ensure you are talking to the decision-maker when you approach a company. Italians like to do business with people they already know.
2. Take a little time getting to know each other, but meetings are for conducting business. Start meetings with a little general conversation to put everyone at ease. In the north, business is often conducted 'time efficiently'.
3. Business is not usually conducted over lunch or dinner.
4. Take your time and be patient. Trying to hurry things along indicates a point of weakness, and you may concede to demands with their promises of a 'quick fix'.
5. Decisions about you/your product will be made away from any formal meetings or negotiations, usually informally during breaks or over lunch with colleagues. The meeting is used to ratify decisions made privately.
6. The Italians won't give you a direct 'No'. They will indirectly convey their lack of interest or dislike.

7. The machismo culture means pride and honour are important in all walks of life. Give and expect respect.
8. Don't use humour and jokes in business. This is deemed inappropriate.
9. Don't mix business with pleasure. The Italians live life to the full, but business is business, and socialising is for enjoying yourself. Italians do not take work home.
10. Don't be surprised when you reach an agreement with Italians that they bring in new demands at the end.

Public holidays

January 1	New Year's Day
January 6	Epiphany
February 1	Venice Carnival starts
February 12	Venice Carnival ends
March/April	Easter Sunday/Monday (date changes every year)
April 25	Venice (St Mark)**
April 25	Liberation Day
May 1	May Day
June	Sunday nearest second Anniversary of the Republic
June 24	Florence (St John)**
June 24	Turin (St John)**
June 29	Rome (Sts Peter and Paul)**
July 11	Palermo (St Rosalia)**
August 15	Assumption of the Blessed Virgin Mary
September 19	Naples (St Gennaro)**
October 4	Bologna (St Petronio)**
November 1	All Saints' Day

November	Sunday nearest fourth Second World War Victory Anniversary Day
December 7	Milan (St Ambrose)**
December 8	Immaculate Conception
December 25	Christmas Day
December 26	Second Day of Christmas or St Stephen's Day

**Feast days

| Weekend | Saturday afternoon, Sunday |
| Business hours | 8.30–12.45 and then 4.30–7.30 (Saturdays 8.30–12.45) |

Celebrations
Second Sunday in May Mother's Day

Norway

1. Warm-hearted good people with a sense of humour. Like to be seen as good hosts and generous.
2. Always be punctual, this is seen as giving respect.
3. Values, ethics, and hard-work drive their businesses.
4. Great respecters of the value and contribution of all employees; they are a joy to work for (so say many foreigners).
5. Expertise and initiative are respected.
6. Norwegians speak bluntly, assertively and are straight-talking. Avoid being confrontational. Assertiveness is respected.
7. Good in committees; give reasoned, educated and well-argued comments.
8. Seen as docile by other more aggressive non-European cultures.
9. Don't criticise other people/cultures too much. The

Norwegians are exceptionally tolerant of other people's values, though they may be frustrated at other cultures' work practices.

10. Don't waste their time. Norwegians are very pragmatic and like to get the job done.

Public holidays

January 1	New Year's Day
March/April	Palm Sunday
March/April	Holy Thursday/Good Friday/Easter Sunday/Easter Monday
May 1	May Day
May 17	National Independence Day
May	Ascension Day (sixth Thursday after Easter)
May/June	Whit Sunday and Monday (Pentecost)
December 24	Christmas Eve (half day)
December 25	Christmas Day
December 26	Boxing Day
December 31	New Year's Eve (half day)
Weekend	Saturday, Sunday
Business hours	8.00–4.00 (3.00 on Fridays)

Spain

1. A personal contact who can help you cultivate business relationships is a must. Spaniards value personal influence and it is difficult to accomplish anything on your own.

2. Be formal when first meeting people, use titles, and show respect to seniors.

3. Small talk and 'taking measure' requires a long time before you can get down to any business dealings. Success depends on personal rapport. You may need

several 'sniffing' meetings.

4. Relationships may appear informal, but there is a formality at heart based on pride, honour, and trust. Always remember to introduce people to the most senior Spaniard first.

5. All correspondence should be formal.

6. Spaniards enjoy '*disfrutar*' time, not spend it or waste it. Time is very fluid. Lots of business is conducted in bars and restaurants, over good wine and 'cognac'.

7. Appeal to the emotions of a Spaniard, but have some facts and substance to back this up. They are very visual and imaginative with their use of language. Translate documents into Spanish.

8. Don't put a Spaniard in a position of losing face: remember they are a machismo culture of pride and honour.

9. Don't impose deadlines; you will be disappointed and frustrated, and you will give out signals that Spaniards are untrustworthy.

10. Don't believe mañana means tomorrow – it means 'not today'.

Public holidays
The seven national holidays and five widely celebrated other holidays are listed below.

1 January	New Year's Day (*Día del Año Nuevo*)*
6 January	Epiphany or Holy Kings' Day (*Día de los Reyes Magos*)
19 March	St Joseph's Day (*Día de San José*)
March/April	Good Friday (*Viernes Santo*)* date changes every year

1 May	Labour Day (*Día del Trabajador*)*
Ascension Day	Sixth Thursday after Easter
May	Whit Sunday (Pentecost: seventh Sunday after Easter)
May/June	Corpus Christi: second Thursday after Pentecost
25 July	St. James' Day (*Día de Santiago*)
15 August	Assumption of the Virgin (*Asunción*)*
12 October	Virgin of Pilar or National Day (*Día de Virgen del Pilar*)*
8 December	Immaculate Conception (*Inmaculada Concepción*)*
25 December	Christmas Day (*Día de Navidad*)*

* National Holidays (in addition there are two local holidays allowed).

Weekend	Sunday
Business hours	9.00–1.30 and then 3.00/4.00–6.00/ 7.00 (summer 8.30–2.30)

Things to be aware of
When a public holiday falls on a Tuesday or Thursday, a four day holiday is taken – called building a bridge (*puente*). If a holiday falls on a Wednesday it's common for employees to take the two preceding/succeeding days off – called building a viaduct (*viaducto*). When two public holidays fall midweek, many people take the whole week off – called *superpuente*.

Sweden
1. Business is a serious matter – they won't waste your

time and you must not waste theirs.
2. Compared with other Nordic countries Swedish decision-making takes a long-time. Everybody should be involved in a consensus decision.
3. Bragging and posturing seems pushy and unseemly. You should be modest and low-key in your style.
4. They like concrete data, facts and evidence, so avoid frills and hyperbole in your presentations. Don't expect the Swedes to use their imagination – you must do it for them.
5. Swedes get straight down to business with no small talk.
6. Swedes are casual, but reserved. They don't think humour is appropriate in business situations.
7. Quality of life is important. Swedes will take their coffee/lunch breaks and go home on time; therefore, the pace of business seems to be relaxed.
8. Be punctual at all times; tardiness is seen as disrespectful.
9. Don't be confrontational; this makes Swedes very uncomfortable.
10. Don't be frightened by silence; silence is part of their communication.

Public holidays

January 1	New Year's Day
January 5	Eve of Epiphany (banks close early)
January 6	Epiphany
March/April	Maundy Thursday (half day) day before Good Friday
March/April	Good Friday (date changes every year)

March/April	Easter Sunday/Monday
April 30	Valborg's Eve (banks close early)
May 1	May Day
Ascension Day	Sixth Thursday after Easter (officially one day but often two)
May	Whit Sunday/Monday Pentecost: seventh Sunday after Easter
June 6	National Day – some public sector employees only
June	Friday before Midsummer Day Midsummer's Eve (bank holiday)
June	Saturday after 19 Midsummer Day
November	Friday before All Saints' Day All Saints Eve (banks close early)
November	First Saturday after 30 October All Saints' Day
December 24	Christmas Eve (bank holiday)
December 25	Christmas Day
December 26	Second Christmas Day
December 31	New Year's Eve (bank holiday)
Weekend	Saturday, Sunday
Business hours	8.30/9.00–5.00

Things to be aware of
The evening before a holiday is as important as the holiday itself. Most Swedes have half the day off to prepare for the evening.

Celebrations

February 14	St Valentine's Day
April 1	April Fools' Day
May	Last Sunday Mothers' Day

November	Second Sunday Father's Day
December 10	Nobel Day (flags are flown)
December 13	St Lucia Day (early morning celebrations)

United Kingdom

1. There is still some hierarchy in British firms, with a distinctive difference between the status of executives and managers, with most executives having secretaries.
2. Use titles and formal address until invited to do otherwise. There is a generation gap concerning this; anyone under 35 will use first names.
3. British business people take their time making decisions. Allow them time to think things over. However, once a decision is made you can expect implementation to start.
4. Although a lot of business communication is done orally, send or leave detailed information about your company, and a summary of the meeting/phone call just conducted.
5. Communication is open, direct, impersonal and detailed. It can be contradictory; but it should never be personal.
6. Understatement is very common. Brits hate over emphasis (hyperbole), they see it as boastful and pushy. Sometimes Brits appear less enthusiastic than they really are.
7. Presentations are structured and formal, but usually have an element of humour. Nowadays, an element of entertainment is expected. The audience will expect to ask questions at the end.

8. Although English is spoken all over the world, many cultures need an interpreter to understand if the British are saying 'Yes'. Wanting always to be polite, and to have time to think, a standard business response is, 'We'll think about it.'
9. Don't give British people a 'hard sell' or an 'American sell'. They dislike it, seeing it as manipulative and pushy. They'll walk away.
10. Don't propose drastic changes or fast timings. They find both uncomfortable. Remember! They need time to think things over.

Public holidays

January 1	New Year's Day
March/April	Good Friday (date changes every year)
March/April	Easter Sunday/Monday
May	Bank holiday: first Monday of May
May	Spring Bank holiday: last Monday of May
August	Summer Bank holiday: last Monday of August
December 25	Christmas Day
December 26	Boxing Day
Weekend	Saturday, Sunday
Business hours	9.00–5.30

Scotland also celebrates:

January 2	(New Year's Bank holiday)
Summer	Bank holiday (first Monday of August)

But doesn't celebrate:

Easter Monday
Spring Bank holiday (last Monday of May)

Northern Ireland also celebrates:
March 17   St Patrick's Day
July 12   Orangeman's Day

Celebrations:
Mother's Day   Second Sunday of March
Father's Day   Third Sunday of June
November 5   Guy Fawkes' Day (Bonfire Night)

THE FAR EAST

People in the Far East are *not* casual so be very respectful of their way of dressing; if you do not conform they will think you are being disrespectful. The Chinese have seven layers of wrapping presents, so wrapping *you* should be equally important – it's all about *face*. The dominant feature of business practice is your personal network: based on duty, obligation and trust.

China

1. You need to establish a network of close contacts with personal ties. This *guanxi* is your key to success.
2. Respect and trust must be earned before business can be negotiated. Expect to take five years in the build up.
3. Don't be impatient you will usually be met with delays.
4. In business dealings, be detailed, technical and factual. Speak often of trust and co-operation between you and your counterparts. Focus on long-term benefits.
5. Chinese negotiators use the 'soft sell' and the 'hard

buy'. A 'no compromise' approach is used, but flexibility eventually emerges; ensure you have plenty of room to give lots of concessions. Expect shaming and silence as negotiations tactics.

6. Always give notice upfront about your full intentions and what you want to achieve in China. This is not only considered a courtesy, but shows your intentions are honourable.

7. Never send one individual into negotiations, nor a lawyer. Chinese prefer to deal with groups. Have technically competent engineers and other experts on your team.

8. Don't say anything that might embarrass your counterpart; remember face! Be subtle and sensitive in your disagreements and try not to ask direct questions which might need 'No' for an answer.

9. Don't upset the harmony. Be reserved and dignified in your personal style.

10. Don't expect quick decision-making. The hierarchy within a Chinese organisation is complicated. It is often difficult to identify who makes the final decision, but everyone along the way will need to 'rubber stamp' their agreement.

Public holidays

January 1–2	New Year's Day Holiday
February 12–16	Chinese New Year
March 8	International Women's Working Day*
May 1–2	International Labour Day
May 4	Youth Day
June 1	Children's Day

July 1	Anniversary of the Founding of the Communist Party
August 1	Anniversary of the Founding of the Chinese PLA
October 1-2	National Day

*Holiday for women only

| Weekend | Sunday |
| Business hours | 8.00–5.00 |

Non-holiday observances

April 5	*Qing Ming*
June 25	*Tuen Ng* (Dragon Boat) Festival
October 1	Mid-Autumn Festival

Japan

1. Creating harmony (*Wa*) is the overriding criterion for any transaction.
2. Business is done through your personal network (*Nemawashi*).
3. Expect to spend a long time building relationships and a network. You will be asked questions about your personal background and education, ask the same questions about them; this communicates your interest in them on a long-term basis.
4. Asking for and accepting help, even when not needed, and giving help are all means to create trust and *Wa*.
5. Decisions must go through the *Ringey sho* process; approval by everyone. A decision may be ages in the making, but implementation is swift.
6. Repeat questions several times. Silence is respectful. Closed eyes are a sign of concentration – not sleep!
7. Be prepared for lots of formality and documents.

THE TEN BEST TIPS FOR DOING BUSINESS AROUND THE WORLD / **217**

8. Don't put anyone in a position where they might lose face.
9. Don't ask direct questions and don't interrupt.
10. Don't think people are lying if you feel misled; remember there is no 'No'.

Public holidays

January 1	New Year's Day (*Gantan*)
January 2	Bank Holiday
January 3	Bank Holiday
January	Second Monday Coming of Age Day (*Seijin-no-hi*)
February 11	National Foundation Day (*Kenkoku-kinen-no-hi*)
March 21	Vernal Equinox (*Shunbun-no-hi*)
April 29	Greenery Day (*Midori-no-hi*)
May 3	Constitution Memorial Day (*Kenpou-kinen-bi*)
May 4	Holiday for a Nation (*Kokumin-no-kyujitu*)
May 5	Children's Day (*Kodomo-no-hi*)
July 20	Marine Day (*Umi-no-hi*)
September 15	Respect for the Aged Day (*Keirou-no-hi*)
September 23	Autumnal Equinox (*Shuubun-no-hi*)
October	Second Monday Health and Sports Day (*Taiiku-no-hi*)
November 3	National Culture Day (*Bunka-no-hi*)
November 23	Labour Thanksgiving Day (*Kinrou-kansha-no-hi*)
December 23	Emperor's Birthday (*Tennou-tanjyou-bi*)

December 31   Bank Holiday

Other relevant information
Holidays on a Sunday are taken on the Monday (except Bank Holidays associated with the New Year).
29 April to 5 May (approx.) is called 'Golden Week'. Many people extend the public holidays taking extra days off and most organisations are closed.

Weekend   Saturday afternoon, Sunday
Business hours   9.00–5.00 (Saturdays 9.00–noon)

Myanmar (Burma)

1. Who you know matters a lot, and good connections are necessary to do business.
2. The tradition of repaying favours applies strongly. You are expected to return a favour without being asked.
3. Know people's status, rank and title. Use correct names and formal titles, especially when dealing with government officials.
4. Exchanging business cards is an important transaction.
5. Huge acceptance of authority. The boss is there to make the decisions.
6. Egalitarianism is perceived as a threat to harmony.
7. People won't use their initiative; they'll be waiting for an OK from their superior.
8. Maintain your composure at all times.
9. Don't be surprised that astrologers are used in the decision-making process, or prior to business negotiations.
10. Don't expect a good input in discussions; the

Myanmars are uncomfortable on committees because governance is by seniority or hierarchy.

Public holidays

January 4	Independence Day (1948)
February 12	Day of the Burmese Union
February 23	*Eid al Adha*
March 2	Peasant's Day
March 27	Day of the Army
May 1	Labour Day
July 19	Martyr's Day
December 6	*Eid ul Fitr*
December 25	Christmas Day
Weekend	Saturday, Sunday
Business hours	7.30–4.30

Buddhist events

April	Thingyan Water festival
April	Myanmar New Year
May	Full moon day of Kason, Birth and First Sermon of Buddha
July	Buddhist Fast begins
October	Buddhist Fast ends (Light festival)
November	Tazaungdaing, Full moon, (Light festival, Cloth weaving competition)
November	National Holiday
December\January	Kayin New Year

Things to be aware of
The months are dependent on waxing and waning of the moon. There are 12 months per year; 29 and 30 days duration alternately.

Myanmar calendar	Gregorian calendar
Kason	April and May
Nayon	May and June
Waso	June and July
Wagaung	July and August
Tawthalin	August and September
Thadingyut	September and October
Tazaungmon	October and November
Nadaw	November and December
Pyatho	December and January
Tabodwe	January and February
Tabaung	February and March
Tagu	March and April

Singapore

1. Speed of business is quite quick; quicker than other south east Asian countries. Allow two weeks in advance to make appointments.
2. Although quite 'western' in business outlook, there is still a fundamental belief in harmony in any business relationships.
3. Negotiations are usually direct and quick.
4. Business environment is very entrepreneurial and dynamic.
5. Emphasis on competence, merit and team play.
6. Age and experience are valued, so send people around the age of 50 to do business. This shows seriousness of your intent.
7. Agreements are written down. Singaporeans consider written contracts more binding than verbal agreements.
8. Don't be aggressive in your negotiating.

9. Don't be too 'posturing', this is seen as being pushy.
10. Don't put someone in a position where they might lose face.

Public holidays

January 1	New Year's Day
February 12–14	Chinese New Year
February 23	*Hari Raya Haji* (*Eid Al Adha*)
March/April	Good Friday (date changes every year)
May 1	Labour Day
August 9	National Day
December 25	Christmas Day
Weekend	Sunday (Friday is the Muslim holy day)
Business hours	Generally 9.00–5.00 and half day on Saturday. Lunch 12.00–2.00

Vietnam

1. Personal contacts are crucial. Establish trust and friendship before attempting any business.
2. Wait for a signal from your hosts before talking business.
3. If using a translator, focus your eyes and attention on the person with whom you are meeting, not the translator. Always have your own interpreter present.
4. Learning a few words in Vietnamese, and a little about their country, shows respect, sensitivity and a willingness to do serious business.
5. Start from absolute basics, make no assumptions. Your counterpart will not fill in any missing information or correct misinformation. Make sure that you

understand every item in your contract.

6. Courtesy is important; don't cause someone to lose face, especially in front of his/her peers.

7. Vietnam is a big bureaucracy, everything takes a long time. This can also be used as a tactic in breaking down negotiations or to cause delays.

8. Make it clear that you will not continue negotiations beyond your deadline otherwise delay will be used as a bargaining tool.

9. Don't display emotion; it's considered inappropriate to a business setting. Remember that the Vietnamese display great patience and little emotion in public.

10. Don't show anger or frustration even as a tactic.

Public holidays

January 1	Solar New Year's Day (Bank Holiday)
January 12–14	Vietnamese New Year, *Tet Nguyen Dan*
February 3	Anniversary of the Founding of the Communist Party (Bank Holiday)
March 8	Women's Day
March 26	Youth Day
April 30	Liberation of Ho Chi Minh City (Saigon)
May 1	International Labour Day
May 19	Vietnamese leader Ho Chi Minh's birthday
June 1	Children's Day
July 27	Memorial Day for War Martyrs
August 19	Revolution of 1945
September 2	National Day

November 20   Teachers' Day
December 22   Army Day

Weekend   Saturday, Sunday
Business hours   7.30–4.30

THE MIDDLE EAST

The Middle East comprises Iran, eight Arab states (all Muslim), and Israel (Jewish). The Lebanon refers to itself as an Arab country but is half Arab and half Christian.

The Muslim world is a very strict society and it is essential that you observe Islamic politeness and decorum. The United Arab Emirates are less strict and very cosmopolitan; though still adhere to Muslim values. Segregation of the sexes is an important feature of the Arab world. Men - **do not** under any circumstances touch an Arab woman or give her direct eye contact. No one should behave in public in a flirtatious or affectionate manner – not even married couples. Alcohol is prohibited in most parts of the Middle East and gambling is considered evil.

Women must always be very modestly and conservatively dressed, often covered fully by a *burka* (a long black coat, with or without a veil). Skirts below the knee, high collars and long sleeves are required. You should check on any practice regarding wearing a long scarf for hair cover. There are special areas for westerners where 'normal' dress, behaviour and customs are allowed out of sight of the locals. The United Arab Emirates (Dubai) and The Lebanon (Beirut) are the exceptions; they accept 'western' dress and behaviour.

Israel

1. Israelis speak bluntly, assertively and honestly, demonstrating their respect for you; i.e. you can take straightforward discussions.
2. Very adept at strategic planning, they will try to guess your next move. Assume they know your game plan and be prepared with answers and new tactics.
3. They want action, rather than empty words. Ask for 'time to think' if things are moving a little too quickly for you.
4. Assertiveness is respected if you stand by what you think is right. Stick up for yourself and you should find they will compromise.
5. They appear very, very argumentative.
6. Israelis are experienced negotiators. They are known for being tough but fair.
7. Bargaining starts with high ideals, extreme positions, and moves towards 'compromise'.
8. Keep written agreements short, but always finish up with one.
9. Don't use 'high sounding' or impressive rhetoric. Communication is open, direct, and to the point. Use concise and explicit language.
10. Don't be surprised if your plans have to change. The Israelis are a spontaneous people, so be adaptable.

Public holidays

January 28	*Tu B'Shevat* (New Year of Trees)
February 26	*Purim* (Feast of Lots)
February 27	*Shushan Purim*
March/April	*Pesach* (Passover)[1] (date changes every year)
April 9	*Yom HaShoah* (Holocaust Memorial

	Day)*
April 16	*Yom Hazikaron* (Soldiers' Memorial Day)*
April 17	*Yom Ha Atzmaut* (Independence Day)**
April 30	*Lag B'Omer*
May 10	*Yom Yerushalayim* (Jerusalem Day)
May 17	*Shavuot* (Giving of the Torah)**
July 18	*Tisha B'Av* (Fast of 9 Av)*
September 7–8	*Rosh Hashana* (New Year)**
September 16	*Yom Kippur* (Atonement Day)**
September 21–27	*Sukkot* (Feast of Tabernacles)[1]
September 28	*Shemini Atzeret* and *Simchat Torah*
November 30/ December 5	*Hannukah* (Festival of Lights)

[1]The first and last days of *Sukkot* and *Pesach* are national holidays.
*Most stores and restaurants close.
**National holiday, everything closes.

Weekend	Friday afternoon, Saturday
Business hours	8.00–4.00 (Fridays 8.00–1.00)

Things to be aware of
The Jewish day begins at sundown (6 pm) The feast itself begins at sundown on the day preceding the date shown and ends at sundown on the date shown. Banks and most businesses are closed during all major Jewish holidays. There is no public transportation except for taxis.

Kuwait

1. Subjective feelings are the only way of knowing real truth; facts and evidence are unimportant. Informa-

tion that does not reflect Islamic values is rejected. Solutions to all problems lie in the correct interpretation and application of divine law.

2. Behave in a calm and respectful manner; don't be loud or obtrusive. Maintain plenty of eye contact with your host.

3. Public life is almost entirely the exclusive domain of men (10% of the workforce are women).

4. You will need a letter of introduction to make an appointment. Be prepared for up to three polite-small-talk meetings before you can start any business dealings. Business cards are of immense importance.

5. No privacy in meetings – and these will be constantly interrupted. Muslims take time to pray five times a day. Serving coffee signals the meeting is being brought to an end.

6. A sign of power and superiority will be to keep you (the supplicant) waiting which can be for hours. Negotiations and decisions take hours. Silence is part of this process.

7. Contracts should be as brief as possible and written in Arabic (with an English translation as necessary). Hire a Kuwaiti lawyer.

8. Don't assume the person asking all the questions is the decision-maker. He is usually an unimportant underling.

9. Don't consider making more than one appointment per day.

10. Don't get upset if you have to keep on repeating your message or presentation; it is common practice to ask this for the people who wander into your meeting.

Public holidays

January 1   New Year's Day

February	*Eid Al Adha* (date changes every year)
February 25	National Day
February 26	Liberation Day
March 5	Islamic New Year
May 14	Prophet's Birthday
September 24	*Lailat Al Miraj*
November	*Eid Al Fitr* (date changes every year)
Weekend	Friday
Business hours	Traditionally 7.30/8.30–2.30 and 4.30–8.30

The Lebanon

1. Lebanese are hospitable, easy going and expect personal relationships to develop in their business transactions.
2. A very 'western' country with underlying 'Arab' features; strong family, socialising and hospitality overlaid with French logic and style, and American sense of achievement.
3. Warm greetings, handshakes, and questions about family and health are usual when meeting someone. Use titles and formality at first.
4. How you *look* is *very* important. Your clothes, hair and jewellery all make a statement about you – more than your competence or credentials.
5. Many women work and want to be regarded as equals.
6. Expect your Lebanese counterpart to arrive a little late for a meeting. Lots of small talk is the preamble to conducting business.
7. American dollars are used as easily as local currency. French is the second language and English the third.

8. Don't expect things to happen quickly. Decisions are taken slowly whilst relationships build.
9. Don't impose deadlines – you'll disappoint yourself and get frustrated!
10. Don't criticise anything directly; suggest/hint you would like changes.

Public holidays

There are six Muslim and six Christian national holidays taken by all along with several non-denominational holidays.

January 1	New Year's Day
January 6	Christmas (Armenian community)
January 7	Christmas (Orthodox)
February 9	St Maroon's Day
February 12	*Eid Al Adha*
March 5	Islamic New Year
March/April	Good Friday/Easter/Easter Monday (Western/Orthodox on different dates)
May 1	Labour Day
May 6	Martyr's Day
May 14	Prophet's Birthday
August 15	Assumption
September 24	*Lailat al Miraj*
October 25	*Ashoora*
November 1	All Saints' Day
November 22	Independence Day
November 26	*Eid Al Fitr*
December 25	Christmas Day
Weekend	Sunday (Friday Muslim holy day)
Business hours	8.00–6.00

Saudi Arabia

1. The strictest of all Arab nations; you need to obey their rules.
2. If you are a woman, don't go – (a Kuwaiti man's advice to Deborah). Women are segregated in everything. Expect to be clothed from head to foot, chaperoned, and not be allowed to drive a car. As a business woman, if you are given a visa, there will be little you will be allowed to do.
3. The Saudis are very nationalistic; even other Arabs are *foreigners*, but are more tolerated than (in descending order) Europeans, Philippinos, Indians/Pakistanis.
4. Large hierarchy with Saudis always in the middle to top positions. Only the boss has the right to make a decision.
5. All documents should be dated in Islamic and Gregorian (western) dates.
6. Everything stops or closes during the time of prayers. Saudis are forbidden to work more than six hours per day.
7. Meetings are frequently interrupted. They take place early morning or after sundown, up to midnight.
8. Be very sensitive to their traditions.
9. Don't be surprised if a Saudi 'queue jumps'; he is entitled to come before any foreigners.
10. Don't expect expertise to count in the decision-making process. Governance is by superiority and hierarchy.

Public holidays
The Islamic Hijrah calendar is 12 months x 28 days – therefore, public holidays fall on a different 'western'

calendar date each year.

February	*Eid Al Adha* (3 days)
September	Unification of the Kingdom
November	*Eid Al Fitr* (3 days)
Weekend	Thursday, Friday
Business hours	7.30/8.30–2.30 (and possibly 5.00–7.00)

Things to be considered
Non-Muslims need to be invited or sponsored to enter the country. You need an exit permit to leave the country, whatever the emergency.

United Arab Emirates

1. Respect and friendship must be reached before any negotiations can take place.
2. All contracts should be translated into English and Arabic. Contracts may be broken at any time, justified because you are not a Muslim. However, trust and friendship will seal a true bond.
3. Bargaining is part of the process of negotiation. Start with high demands and then work your way towards a 'compromise'.
4. Nothing gets hurried. Be patient. Time is flexible. Deadlines are nothing more than approximations. Transactions may take a long time to finalise.
5. Decisions are made by a few principal people at the top of the company.
6. Business people prefer to deal with the same people throughout, so keep the same negotiating team.
7. Don't submit a report of seven pages or so; 57 is more to their liking! Lots of paper and documentation is

seen as serious 'meat'.

8. Don't get upset when your business meetings are constantly interrupted; this is the way of life, not a signal that you are unimportant.
9. Don't be aggressive in your attitude or demand 'Yes' or 'No' answers.
10. Don't underestimate the significance of social gatherings; many business transactions are dealt with then.

Public holidays

January 1	New Year's Day
February 23	*Eid Al Adha*
March 15	Islamic New Year
May 25	Prophet's Birthday
August 6	H.H. Sheikh Zayed Bin Sultan Al Nahyan's Accession Day
October 5	*Lailat al Miraj*
November	Start of *Ramadan* (not a holiday) (date changes every year)
December 2	National Day
December 6	*Eid Al Fitr*
Weekend	Thursday/Friday or Friday/Saturday
Business hours	8.30–1.00 and then 2.30–6.00 (some 7.30–4.00)

Things to be aware of

The Dubai Shopping Festival takes place each year during the month of March.

October is conference month and hotels are fully booked.

As a Muslim country, things may stop for prayers (12.30 and 20.00 for half an hour)

NORTH AMERICA

The United States and Canada are two very different countries. However, they both value independence and action, and they are geared to a highly paced change. Achievement of personal goals, wealth and prestige are driving factors for them. Canadians are much more interested in substance and facts, and are serious about content and purpose. Canadians view themselves as the 'younger brother' to the USA.

Canada

1. Two different languages and two different cultural backgrounds; French and English. Business attitudes and behaviours differ between the Anglo-/Franco-parts of Canada.

2. Business communication tends to be more formal in Ontario and Atlantic Canada than in Québec and the West. When dealing with French Canadians have all documents translated into French.

3. Eye contact and smiles are very important.

4. Business is not as quick paced as in the US.

5. You need to be clear, concise, and *thorough* in all your business dealings.

6. You will be respected for logical, well-argued positions. The Canadians are very analytical.

7. They drive a hard bargain, but are not as aggressive as their US counterparts.

8. US-style efficiency and effectiveness dominate business, but this is overridden by long-term gains, not short-term results.

9. Don't use first names unless invited to do so. Canadians are quite formal.

10. Don't assume Canadians are like Americans. They are more conservative, formal at the outset, and not such great risk takers.

Public holidays

January 1	New Year's Day
March/April	Good Friday/Easter Sunday/Easter Monday
May 19	Victoria Day
July 1	Canada Day
August	First Monday, civic or provincial holidays
September 1	Labour Day
October 13	Thanksgiving
November 11	Remembrance Day
December 25	Christmas Day
December 26	Boxing Day
Weekend	Saturday, Sunday
Business hours	10.00–6.00

United States of America

1. The American style is competitive and even aggressive. To them it is more important to win and be seen as a winner, than to appear conciliatory. Therefore match their style with a confident bearing, and be prepared to 'cut to the chase' without delay.
2. Although their style is aggressive and abrasive, it should not be taken personally. Americans are paradoxically sensitive about personal abuse. Also, they are uncomfortable with the use of emotion in negotiations.
3. Their style is direct and to the point, with sustained

eye contact. They say what they mean and mean what they say. Don't think of them as Anglo-Saxon, but rather as out-going Germans.

4. American deals are all about the 'bottom line' – profitability. And quick results. They want a short pay-back time, and will take risks in line with that attitude.

5. They will not hold on to declining fortunes. They make quick decisions to go in...and to get out.

6. They want every agreement confirmed in writing – and every proposal too. Nothing is binding until both parties have signed their agreement.

7. They are hot on detail so contracts should be drawn up with a lawyer's assistance. Americans will insist on contracts being carried out as agreed.

8. When they show irritation or even anger during negotiations, it is not personal but related only to the matter being discussed.

9. They are embarrassed but unimpressed by signs of vulnerability in negotiations, just like the Germans.

10. They believe in winning, so let your first offer contain enough room for manoeuvre, and expect a hard bargaining session.

Public holidays

January 1	New Year's Day
January 20	Inauguration Day (President installed)
January 3	Martin Luther King Jr Day
February 3	Presidents' Day/Washington's birthday
May	Memorial Day (last Monday)

July 4	Independence Day
September 1	Labour Day
October 2	Columbus Day
November 11	Veterans' Day
November 4	Thanksgiving Day
December 25	Christmas Day

Weekend	Saturday and Sunday
Business hours	8.30/9.00–5.00/6.00

Non-holiday observances or celebrations

January 20	Inauguration Day occurs each fourth year starting from 1965
February 2	Groundhog Day
February 14	Valentine's Day
March 17	St Patrick's Day
April 1	April Fools' Day
June 14	Army Day
April 22	Earth Day
April	Wednesday of last full week Administrative Professional's Day
May 6	Nurses' Day
May	First Thursday National Day of Prayer
May	Second Sunday Mothers' Day
May	Third Saturday Armed Forces Day
June	Third Sunday Fathers' Day
June 19	Liberation of Slaves
July	Fourth Sunday Parents' Day
August 1	Air Force Day
August 4	Coast Guard Day
August	First Sunday Friendship Day
September	Sunday after Labour Day

	Grandparents' Day
September 17	Citizenship Day or Constitution Day
October	Second Sunday National Children's Day
October 6	Bosses' Day
October	(Third Saturday) Sweetest Day
October 26	Mother-in-Law's Day
October 27	Navy Day
October 31	Halloween
November 10	Marine Corps Day
December 7	Pearl Harbor Remembrance Day
December 26–31	*Kwanzaa* (African-American cultural holiday)

RUSSIA

A vast country, peopled by many ethnic groups, with its culture deeply rooted in traditions from the East and West. Russians have an egalitarian work ethic and are suspicious of those who 'make good'. There is a general distrust of authority after years of autocratic rule. Many things are still in short supply but can be obtained on the black market. People still talk about the intelligentsia, and visits to the opera and ballet are common in all walks of life.

1. Getting an invitation letter and visa can be a lengthy process; it is often quicker to obtain a tourist visa.
2. Bribery is on the increase in the new market economy and many minor officials expect 'commissions'.
3. You are better making a personal approach than the 'hard sell'. Russians have a strong spirit and passion (their emotional soul, *dusha*) which are expressed frequently.

4. They adopt a hard line in negotiating. Compromise is seen as a weakness and is morally incorrect; they will walk out of negotiations rather than give in. They are patient in waiting for concessions and will 'out-sit' the opposing team.

5. Present in writing everything you hope to do and achieve (long-term aims) in any business venture. Present total unity among your team. Study and agree all details before signing any contract; once signed further negotiations are not allowed.

6. A *protokol* is a written summary of the day's meeting; you will be asked to sign this. This is not an agreement, merely a list of events.

7. Russians like status, good international connections, and academic credentials. Be sure to mention yours and include any relevant information on your business cards (which should be bilingual). A network of well-connected close friends is of great importance.

8. Don't be calm; Russians expect you to be highly emotional, proclaim the deal is off, and to walk out of negotiations! Hold out for more attractive terms.

9. Don't assume people are telling lies; the practice of *Vranyo* (telling fibs) is very common (the Russian form of posturing). Making out to be prosperous and full of potential is part of this – appearances can be deceiving.

10. Don't expect your counterparts to be punctual; they may arrive one or two hours late for an appointment. Patience not punctuality is considered a virtue!

Public holidays

January 1   New Year's Day

January 2	Second Day of New Year
January 7	Christmas Day
February 23	Defenders of the Motherland
March 8	International Women's Day
March/April	Easter Sunday
May 1	Labour Day/Spring Festival (two days)
May 9	Victory Day (Second World War)
June 9	Independence Day
November 7	Day of Accord and Reconciliation
December 12	Constitution Day
Weekend	Saturday, Sunday
Business hours	9.00–5.00

14

Corruption Index

This list was complied by Transparency International; a not-for-profit, non-governmental organisation. The CPI is based on the perceptions of businessmen, risk analysts and the general public on the degree of corruption among public officials and politicians. This is not intended as the definitive indicator, but rather as a guide to relative values.

CPI score range 10 (highly clean) to 0 (highly corrupt)

Place	County	CPI score
1	Finland	9.9
2	Denmark	9.5
3	New Zealand	9.4
4	Iceland	9.2
4	Singapore	9.2
6	Sweden	9.0
7	Canada	8.9
8	Netherlands	8.8
9	Luxembourg	8.7
10	Norway	8.6
11	Australia	8.5
12	Switzerland	8.4
13	United Kingdom	8.3

14	Hong Kong	7.9
15	Austria	7.8
16	Israel	7.6
16	USA	7.6
18	Chile	7.5
18	Ireland	7.5
20	Germany	7.4
21	Japan	7.1
22	Spain	7.0
23	France	6.7
24	Belgium	6.6
25	Portugal	6.3
26	Botswana	6.0
27	Taiwan	5.9
28	Estonia	5.6
29	Italy	5.5
30	Namibia	5.4
31	Hungary	5.3
31	Trinidad & Tobago	5.3
31	Tunisia	5.3
34	Slovenia	5.2
35	Uruguay	5.1
36	Malaysia	5.0
37	Jordan	4.9
38	Lithuania	4.8
38	South Africa	4.8
40	Costa Rica	4.5
40	Mauritius	4.5

42	Greece	4.2
42	South Korea	4.2
44	Peru	4.1
44	Poland	4.1
46	Brazil	4.0
47	Bulgaria	3.9
47	Croatia	3.9
47	Czech republic	3.9
50	Colombia	3.8
51	Mexico	3.7
51	Panama	3.7
51	Slovak Republic	3.7
54	Egypt	3.6
54	El Salvador	3.6
54	Turkey	3.6
57	Argentina	3.5
57	China	3.5
59	Ghana	3.4
59	Latvia	3.4
61	Malawi	3.2
61	Thailand	3.2
63	Dominican Republic	3.1
63	Moldova	3.1
65	Guatemala	2.9
65	Philippines	2.9
65	Senegal	2.9
65	Zimbabwe	2.9
69	Romania	2.8

69	Venezuela	2.8
71	Honduras	2.7
71	India	2.7
71	Kazakhstan	2.7
71	Uzbekistan	2.7
75	Vietnam	2.6
75	Zambia	2.6
77	Cote D'Ivoire	2.4
77	Nicaragua	2.4
79	Ecuador	2.3
79	Pakistan	2.3
79	Russia	2.3
82	Tanzania	2.2
83	Ukraine	2.1
84	Azerbaijan	2.0
84	Bolivia	2.0
84	Cameroon	2.0
84	Kenya	2.0
88	Indonesia	1.9
88	Uganda	1.9
90	Nigeria	1.0
91	Bangladesh	0.4

Index

achievement, 50
Africa, African, 26, 161
agreements, 29
American, USA, 5, 11, 20, 38, 108, 126, 154, 233
Arab, 22, 25
Asia, 171
attitudes, 30, 136, 149
Australia, 176

Bosnia, 186
British/English, 16, 51
business cards, 138

Canada, Canadian, 232
China, Chinese, 32, 35, 60, 69, 157, 214
colloquialisms, 85
Confucius, 34
contracts, 146
corruption, 240
Croatia, Croatian, 5, 187
cultural learning, 63

Denmark, 194

Egypt, 162
emotions, 102

etiquette, 137
Europe, 193

face, 17, 27, 69, 71
Finland/Finns, 44, 72, 81, 89, 105, 115, 122, 155, 196
France, French, 45, 116, 123, 198

Germany, German, 107, 116, 124, 200
good manners, 14
Greece, Greek, 117, 124, 202
greetings, 122
Guatemala, 181

Honduras, 183
humour, 29, 95, 120
Hungary, 189

India, Indian, 7, 22, 68, 72, 171
individuality, 49, 79, 150
Israel, 224
Italy, Italian, 117, 125, 204

Japan, Japanese, 19, 24, 93, 98, 125, 157, 216

Kenya, 163
knowledge transfer, 151
Kuwait, 225

leadership styles, 46
Lebanon, 227

Macedonia, 190
Malawi, 11, 90, 159
Mañana, 25, 78
mangled metaphors, 12
meetings, 28
meetings, international, 133
Mexican, 20
Middle East, 223
mistakes, xiii
Mozambique, 164
Muslim, 22, 53, 223
Myanmar (Burma), 218

negotiation, 140
New Zealand, 180
Nicaragua, 184
Nigeria, 165
no, for Asians, 70, 75
non-white, 7
Norway, Norwegian, 118, 206

Oriental, 9, 17

Pakistan, 173
political correctness, 158
privacy, 48
project management, 153

reasoning, 37, 110

religion, 36, 46
respect, 16, 31, 56, 99
risk taking, 48
Romania, 192
rules, attitude to, 43
Russia, Russian, xvi, 51, 118,
    159, 236

Saudi Arabia, 229
Scandinavian, 62
selling, 154
Senegal, 167
seniority, 15
Singapore, 220
South Africa, 168
Spain, Spanish, 19, 25, 119,
    126, 207
Sri Lanka, 175
status, 47
Sweden, Swedish, 19, 119,
    155, 209

Ten Keys, 13
timekeeping, 25, 28, 99

United Arab Emirates, 230
United Kingdom, 212

values, 31, 53
vicious spiral, 62
Vietnam, 221
virtuous spiral, 59

yes, Oriental style, 73

Zimbabwe, 170